To Lynne

Well Be Back

Best Wishes

Margaret.

Well Be Back

▼

MARGARET MCALPINE

authorHOUSE®

AuthorHouse™ UK Ltd.
1663 Liberty Drive
Bloomington, IN 47403 USA
www.authorhouse.co.uk
Phone: 0800.197.4150

Cover Image: Rachael Imam rcimam@me.com

Published by AuthorHouse   03/29/2014

ISBN: 978-1-4918-9693-8 (sc)
ISBN: 978-1-4918-9741-6 (e)

Contents

Arrival 1

Easter 9

Work.. 19

Findings 26

Murchison..34

Unwelcome Visitors 41

Buwidgee 50

Volunteers 59

Pre-schools...68

Special Needs...75

Container City 83

Celebration 92

Knitting 99

Buliisa 105

Football.. 113

Mango flies 119

Museum... 127

Mixed feelings 134

Disaster 143

And so 147

Arrival

*N*ERVOUS OF MISSING the plane and daunted at the idea of farewells, I arrive at Heathrow Airport two hours before check-in, to find I have mistaken the flight time and have three hours to spare. I settle for a glass of wine and a plate of pasta and try to forget that I can still call a taxi and head back to Suffolk in time for Sunday evening TV.

I check my boarding pass against the departure screens, try to relax and swallow my lasagne. Once on the plane I select 'Pride and Prejudice' as a suitable inflight introduction to Uganda and settle into my seat.

It's too late now to change my mind. I'm leaving the last two years behind—the ovarian cancer, the hysterectomy, chemotherapy and sudden departure of the husband of forty years who, tired of the misery, found himself a younger fitter model and hot footed it to the south west of Ireland.

Thankfully a discreet cough above my head interrupts my train of thought. A smart middle-aged man is leaning over my seat, proffering a hand to be shaken. I offer mine in return and he points to a boy of about twelve standing next to him. He wishes to introduce us he says, with a charming Eastern European accent, because his son is to be my neighbour during the flight. He is sure he will be well behaved. Should there be a problem he and his wife can be found in business class.

The boy sits down and I smile as warmly as possible, wondering how far my responsibilities towards him stretch. Meanwhile he leans forward and rubs his fingers through a curly mop of very dry hair. The rubbing becomes scratching and the scraping of nails on scalp grows increasingly loud. Every so often the noise stops, as he shakes his head wildly in all directions and I move down in my seat to avoid what tumbles out.

Nine hours later he is still scratching and I have joined him.

It's early morning and Lake Victoria shimmers in the sunshine as the plane circles above Entebbe Airport. After months of failing to come to terms with the disintegration of life as I knew it, I have escaped albeit temporarily from drinking, knitting and sending anguished emails to someone who is no longer interested in receiving them.

Six weeks volunteering with Soft Power Education lies ahead of me. I know little about the organisation other than it is small, non-religious and based in the town of Jinja, that it refurbishes government primary schools and funds two pre-school nurseries and an education centre. For me its great attractions are that it comes recommended by someone I trust and it's a long way from home.

To my relief my suitcases appear on the carousel and I hand over the money for my visa to a customs official who enquires politely 'How are you?' and stamps my passport.

'Mag McAlpine'. I spot my name on a piece of A4 paper being waved in the air.

'How are you? How is there? I am Robert.'

My taxi driver greets me with what I later realise is the traditional Ugandan greeting. His English is good although at first I struggle with the unfamiliar accent. Once installed in his clean but aged car, I wonder at the modern road system and high rise buildings. Entebbe looks very like any other modern airport. Less than a mile further on and I see signs of Africa. The road has narrowed and is red and dusty. The lush green of the countryside is spectacular to someone who little more than twelve hours ago was driving through the uniformly grey dregs of an English winter. The modern buildings are replaced by shacks and trading stalls which every so often are painted in startling yellow or bright pink to advertise mobile phone companies or paint shops. Everywhere there are signs advertising schools, nurseries and churches, the latter offering friendship with Jesus and eternal life.

The traffic itself is exotic: minibuses used as matatus or public buses, painted white and blue, crammed with passengers with luggage tied precariously on top. Painted on the back windows are notices proclaiming 'Man United for Ever', 'We support Arsenal' or more soberly, 'Jesus is our saviour'. Cyclists wobble along the road with pieces of furniture or huge bunches of bananas tied on to their saddles and boxes balancing on the handlebars. Adults and children dash from one side of the road to the other in and out of the traffic to the accompaniment of shouts, screeches and horns. It is chaotic and noisy but surprisingly good humoured.

Half an hour out of Entebbe and we approach the urban sprawl that is Kampala, the capital. Built like Rome, on seven hills, the city is impressive from a distance. The skyline is pierced by skyscraper buildings. Standing out on the horizon are the Namirembe cathedral and the Baha'i Temple, the only one in Africa dedicated to a faith with its roots in Persia in the 1850s. On closer view the city is less attractive as modern buildings jostle with ramshackle huts selling clothes, phone cards and vegetables. Along the central reservation are signs announcing optimistically 'Green tea cures AIDS'. There is plenty of time to take in my surroundings as the traffic system is gridlocked through Kampala. Robert points out this regular occurrence is being made worse by a hold-up on the other side of the road. He is right. Armed lorries start to pass us filled with soldiers carrying machine guns, followed by an impressive line of limousines with shaded windows.

The next town en route to Jinja is Mukono which judging from the advertising hoarding is the schools' capital of the world. Everyone is catered for: Little Angels Nursery School, Our Friend the Lord Secondary School, Muslim schools, Catholic schools, boys' schools, girls' schools, boarding schools and day schools—they are all there.

Soon we are in green undulating countryside, peppered by a couple of Chinese factories with dragons guarding the gates, an impressive school which I am told has recently been upgraded to a university, followed by coffee plantations sloping gently down to the road and then fields of sugar cane. According to Robert the sugar cane is causing problems.

There is not enough sugar produced in Uganda, which pushes up the price. The government wants to extend the industry by planting cane in what is now part of the Mabira Forest Reserve. The plan is complicated by the fact that the owners of the sugar company are Indian, which has stirred up some of the old prejudices many Ugandans have about the Indian community. The issue has led to riots in Kampala.

There are also tea plantations bordering the road. Tea is grown as a commercial crop and at one time both coffee and tea were thriving industries. Coffee is still grown by many in their gardens and sold to agents, although prices have plummeted. Tea planting suffered in the unrest of the 1970s and has never fully recovered.

The countryside changes as we reach the Mabira Forest Reserve itself with its tall trees and dense undergrowth. Ravaged for decades for its wild rubber trees, then cleared by landless subsistence farmers during the war years, there is now a strong feeling that the forest must be preserved for its animals, birds and trees and that given sensitive management it could become a major tourist attraction.

By the side of the road are rows of stalls laden with arrangements of pineapples, mangoes, bananas, tomatoes and aubergines. As the car slows down dozens of market traders all dressed in identical blue tabards, rush to the windows bearing plates of cut fruit, skewers loaded with meat lollipops and bottles of water. Robert makes a joke I don't understand, the traders laugh and move back and the car edges forward.

As I nod off, lulled by the heat and sunshine, Robert announces we are approaching Jinja and my stomach lurches at what lies ahead. We cross the impressive bridge over the Owen Falls Dam and reach a large roundabout with a Chinese restaurant on one side and market stalls on the other, with piles of sandals and clothes on the ground, table cloths hanging on poles and joints of meat on hooks. We have left the main Uganda to Kenya road and are headed for the villages of Kyabirwa and Bujagali. Within a few hundred yards the tarmac runs out and the car bumps over clumps of dried red mud, throwing clouds of dust over anyone unfortunate enough to be close by. Children in dazzling school uniforms laugh and jostle each other, nipping around small groups of women with babies tied to their backs and bundles on their heads, avoiding the odd goat, which has slipped its tether and is sitting in the road.

It's down into second gear as we struggle up a steep hill with a Nile Brewery sign at the top. We turn left on to an even more rutted track and finally stop outside a high iron gate. My 'luxury tented accommodation' beckons and I congratulate myself on booking ahead.

I am to experience the pleasure of glamping and intend to enjoy it. I have organised a week in a tent hotel, complete with my own bathroom and a spectacular view across the Nile. Whatever the future holds I have somewhere safe and comfortable to lay my head.

The manager who hails from Yorkshire has a tight smile and a voice like gravel. She loses no time in announcing I can only stay two nights as they are fully booked over Easter. I can come back afterwards but for four nights I am homeless.

'Where can I go?'

She shrugs 'It's Easter. Everywhere's booked.'

'But I thought I was booked in here.'

The toss of the shoulders indicates that the matter is closed. After tomorrow I am on my own. Sitting temporarily in my luxury tent I am at a loss as to what to do. I need to be busy, or I shall sit on my very comfortable bed and have a good cry. Yet it hardly seems worth unpacking. I compromise by sitting outside admiring the view and reading my *Bradt Guide to Uganda*, the tourist Bible, packed full of practical information and fascinating facts.

A couple of hours later there is a volunteers' meeting at Eden Rock, a nearby campsite where I sign up for painting the next day. There are around six of us from Sweden, Ireland, Australia and the UK. Everyone is friendly but centuries younger than me, confident, happy and with roofs over their heads. It's a brief meeting because Shaz the manager is away in Kampala and Cibbi who organises the volunteers on the school refurbishment programme is out painting.

Casually I mention my homeless state, trying to give the impression that while sleeping under a tree holds no terrors for a well travelled, worldly wise woman such as myself, it might be of interest to someone else. A volunteer mentions that our meeting place has dormitories and there might be free beds. Could I cope with sharing a room with twelve or so volunteers forty years younger than me? Worse still could they cope with me? Do I still snore and if I do, how will I know?

Ben and Sonja, the Dutch managers of Eden Rock are lifesavers. Not only do they have beds in the dorm, but they have a banda or small hut free. The previous occupier has gone on safari and in need of money, has indicated he would be happy to sublet.

Safe in the knowledge that I have a bed, I wander off to explore my surroundings. Situated high on the banks of the White Nile, Bujagali is a famous kayaking and rafting spot with a series of hair-raising falls, including one called the Widow Maker. There are two campsites in the village and another in the process of being built. The village itself straggles along the road for around a mile with Eden Rock my new home at one end and the main road at the other. Some homes are built from locally made bricks but many are wattle and daub—a rough framework of woven branches with the gaps between filled with mud. In the centre of the village is a handful of trading stands selling clothes, fruit, chapatis, masks and carvings, phone time and basic foodstuffs. One hut stands out from its neighbours. It is bright pink and on the side is painted: 'Avoid Morning Sex Africa'.

Back in my luxurious tent hotel I delight in telling the manager I shall not be moving back after Easter. I should have saved myself the trouble—the shrug tells me plainly she couldn't care less.

Whatever the failings may be in the booking system, the restaurant is well run and the food reassuringly familiar.

It is here that I meet Claire. Tall and beautiful, lively and confident, with plaited hair extensions twisted elegantly on top of her head, she introduces herself and her colleagues. She lives in a neighbouring village, has done a basic catering course and is planning a career in hospitality. The friendly chat gives spice to the meal and I begin to relax. Many an evening during my stay is spent eating and chatting to Claire whose ambition is to manage her own hotel.

Easter

*T*HE NEXT DAY is painting and I heave myself up into the truck for the ride to the primary school where Soft Power Education is working.

Around ten years ago Uganda's president Yoweri Museveni introduced free universal primary education and the number of children in school more than doubled. The downside was that without sufficient increase in funding, schools could neither afford to build extra classrooms nor to employ additional staff. Many classes have grown to over a hundred pupils and where there is sufficient staff, there is often no room in which to teach. Schools lack funds and are in a state of disrepair, with no latrines, no water supply and a dearth of desks and blackboards.

Formed in 1999 SPE was the brainchild of Hannah Small, a young British woman living in Uganda and working as an overland driver of tourist trucks. She came to know Bujagali well and seeing the state of the local schools, set up a scheme where her passengers could choose to spend a day repairing a local school and make a donation towards the cost of materials. A Buddhist, she is committed to soft power—progress through communication and discussion rather than hard power—the use of arms and force. She named her project Soft Power Education.

Thanks to Hannah's hard work and the way she has inspired so many others, SPE is now a British registered charity and an officially recognised Ugandan Non-Governmental Organisation. It has renovated more than fifty primary schools in the Jinja area, installing water tanks and pit latrines, putting down concrete floors and building new classrooms. It has built and funds two pre-schools primarily for poor children plus an education centre which is attended by over three hundred pupils for sessions of learning through fun. The aim of SPE is always to work in partnership with the local population.

Our arrival at the school is greeted by a stampede of children, laughing and shouting 'Jambo muzungu'.

In charge of the volunteer painting programme is Cibbi who makes sense of the half empty tins of paint and stiff dry brushes left lying in the corner of what seems to be the head teacher's office. Giving out materials he directs us to various classrooms. No problem here, I think.

Sloshing away happily I notice after a short time that the rest of the painters on my wall are using white paint and I am still on the red I had used for the lintel. Covered in embarrassment I revert to the correct colour and create fuschia pink stripes. Cibbi comes to the rescue and moves me outside to paint window frames in what he clearly sees as my signature red.

The class is carrying on inside as we paint and Eithne, an Irish girl I recognise from the meeting is working next to me. Suddenly she slams down her brush and marches round the building to ambush the teacher on his way to break. What she and the others had seen through the window and I had missed, was a girl of around ten being frogmarched to the front of the class and beaten several times with a cane.

'We are not', we hear Eithne shout, 'giving up our time to improve your school while you cane young children. It's abuse and at home you would lose your job over it.'

The teacher looks at a loss to understand her rage. Physical punishment is legal and common in Ugandan schools. Some teachers even appoint monitors to tell tales on their classmates and to carry out beatings. With large class sizes and cramped conditions, with four pupils squashed on to benches designed for two, many teachers regard the cane as the only way to keep order.

I admire Eithne for her stand. Alerted by pupils the head teacher appears, apologises and assures us all that there will be no other such incident. I'm not sure I believe her but a point has been made.

The agreement with each school is that SPE provides free labour and materials, while the parents of the school provide lunch. I sit down to my first African meal of beans, matoki—a type of small banana baked in its leaves, with greens and groundnut sauce. Feeding the volunteer groups means a significant cost for the local community and our meal is a feast compared with what many families will be eating.

The head teacher walks around with a tray of beakers offering us all freshly squeezed passion fruit juice. 'Only eat fruit you peel yourself': the guide book mantra rings through my head. I get up and find my bottle of water, moving as far as possible from the advancing tray. To no avail—the head finds me, puts a beaker in my hand and pauses to watch me drink. It's delicious and reassured by the medication in my bag and aware of the need for good manners, I finish it off.

A teacher shepherds in twenty or so children aged between seven and fifteen. They are going to sing the Ugandan national anthem. We get to our feet and following the locals, I place hand on chest American style. The head teacher's eyes are on me. She sidles over and indicates politely that I have the wrong hand raised to my chest. Worse is to come. We are told it is our turn to sing. Somebody suggests

'God Save the Queen' and is shouted down despite nobody having a better idea.

Eventually we settle on 'London's Burning' splitting ourselves into pairs and shouting over each other's missed notes and stumbling words. The choir claps politely and then sings our sad rendering back to us in perfect harmony. They had not, we are told by their teacher, ever heard it before.

That evening I take a welcome shower. So the water is piped in straight from the River Nile where the locals bathe and do their washing. I know how lucky I am compared with villagers who have no electricity, no sanitation and walk long distances carrying yellow plastic jerry cans to collect their water from standpipes.

Cibbi arrives most evenings to give out the painting programme for the following day and chat to muzungu volunteers, although he must have answered the same questions a hundred times. In his thirties and born on an island on Lake Victoria, he finished secondary education, but university was way beyond his family finances. He is lively and intelligent and full of interesting information.

Almost the first fact I learn is that Uganda is much more a European than an African concept. Locals identify themselves by their tribe, which is quite likely to extend into Kenya, Tanzania, Sudan or Rwanda and within the tribe, by their clan or extended family unit.

I also find out that Cibbi's view of the slave trade is radically different from what I was taught at school. The idea of noble characters such as Wilberforce insisting that slavery was morally wrong, is viewed with scepticism over here. Much more likely, I am told, is that the advent of the industrial revolution made slaves expensive and expendable. Who needs a dozen slaves to feed when they can have a machine?

The meaning of the word muzungu also becomes clear. My first impression was that muzungus were some sort of persecuted group. I had heard the manager of the hotel berating staff about muzungus stealing tents and at the health centre there is a sign saying 'Treatment 5,000 Ugandan shillings—muzungu rates differ'. Now I know that muzungus are white people and when children wave and shout 'Jambo muzungu' they mean 'hello whitey'. I am not sure it's politically correct but it seems friendly and well meant.

Good Friday and SPE holds a barbecue for volunteers and staff. I am tucking into my hamburger when Nicky, who manages the Amagezi Education Centre comes over for a chat.

'Am I happy painting or would I consider doing something else?'

Cibbi has obviously reported my sad efforts.

'There's a project in the offing looking at why so many pupils drop out of primary education in years six and seven. We need the information to apply for grants and the work is scheduled for a US volunteer who arrives on Sunday, but it's probably too much work for a single person to complete in a month. The only problem is that it will involve travelling around on a boda. How do you feel about that?'

Boda-bodas are deadly motor bikes, almost all in a shocking state of disrepair, driven by guys who tout for pillion passengers, drive like maniacs and leave their cargo on the roadside when they fall off.

I hear words come out of my mouth, 'That would be great.'

It's Easter weekend, the first time I have spent Easter away from family for as long as I can remember. On Saturday I am invited to join a group of London lawyers and their families who are spending the holiday 'glamping' at the luxury tent hotel, possibly in what should have been my tent. They are a friendly welcoming lot. Their trip has been organised by a young lawyer called Paul Daniels, a trustee of SPE.

We spend the day at Kyabirwa Primary School where the pupils have given up their holiday to come and entertain the muzungus. Paul has been a regular visitor to the school for several years and is a good friend of Moses the deputy head. In recognition of their friendship Moses has called his youngest son Paul Daniels.

We are shepherded into a classroom packed to capacity with pupils and squeeze into a couple of benches at the front. I am introduced as 'granny' which does my ego no good. I need to look into Botox when I get home. One of the young visitors asks the class how they celebrate birthdays. The question is met by blank incomprehension. We all begin to feel embarrassed especially the poor girl who asked the question. Finally the teacher explains that Ugandans don't celebrate birthdays and many children don't know the exact date of their birth. However she concedes, sensitive to muzungu embarrassment, if a child does know his or her birthday, friends might well sing 'Happy Birthday'.

In the afternoon there is a football match and sports. The lawyers manfully take on the locals, who play in bare feet and thoroughly enjoy thrashing their opponents, so honour is restored. Everyone has a great time except for one visitor aged about seven years with white blonde hair. So fascinated are the Ugandan children by her appearance, that she is constantly mobbed.

The next day is Easter Day. I go to Mass in the Roman Catholic Church in Jinja with Eithne and Loretta.

Eithne is from Co Tipperary and a mad hurling fanatic. When Tip is playing her brother sends her text updates via her mobile phone every fifteen minutes.

Loretta is Australian of Maltese extraction and adores Snicker bars. Her major moan is that there is an added ingredient in African chocolate, which stops it melting in the heat but affects the taste. Just before leaving Sydney Loretta fell deeply in love with Josip. That was before she met a Ugandan guy she quite liked and before Jim came along on a kayaking exercise with the British Army. She now thinks that at twenty six she's not quite ready to settle down.

The church is packed with an overflow crowd outside in the heat. We have the timing wrong so catch half an hour's mass in Luganda, before sitting through the full monty in English.

The singing is amazing, with beautiful strong African voices and the church is ablaze with colour: women dressed in diamante, ribbons, sequins and lace, men standing stiffly in shirts and ties and young children hopping around behind their parents in over sized suits, net dresses and heavy shoes.

I'm very impressed with the priest who tells the congregation that before he realised he had a vocation for the Church he had thought he would marry and had decided that he would only have three children because that was the number which he could afford to feed and educate. This seems brave stuff coming from a Roman Catholic priest and he certainly gains my respect.

After the service we wander into Jinja town, which is almost deserted. The only activity comes from the huge hideous marabou storks nesting on roofs and hovering round rubbish dumps. With their humped black backs, scraggy heads and jowls, they resemble vultures on a bad day and well deserve their nickname of 'undertaker bird'.

We all begin to feel homesick and in an attempt not to dwell on Easter meals of the past, we treat ourselves to lunch in Leo's, Jinja's Indian restaurant. It is packed full of celebrating families and the only empty table is next to a European woman and a young Ugandan. They greet us warmly and explain they are Christians and the woman is sponsoring the young man through school. He was apparently born a Muslim, but sought out his sponsor several years ago saying he wanted to take Jesus as his saviour.

We explain we are with SPE a non-religious outfit and study our menus. Undeterred the young man asks if we are Christian. I cough into my napkin while Eithne and Loretta say they are Catholic. He points out that he has issues with certain aspects of the Catholic Church. When this elicits no response he asks why Loretta and Eithne are working for a non-religious organisation when there is so much of the Lord's work to be done. Eithne seems to have become deaf at this point, which leaves Loretta to explain that she believes people should be free to make up their own minds about what they believe and it is not her job to challenge anyone else's beliefs.

'You are not a Christian' is the reply. 'You are not carrying out the work of the Lord. You have not accepted Christ as your saviour.'

I make a remark about the heat, but am interrupted by the sponsor who smiles fondly at her protegé and says that he loves to debate. Forking away at my biryani I wait for Loretta to tip her goat curry over his crisp white shirt. Luckily they finish before us and he leaves with a final rejoinder that Loretta should rethink her godless ways.

What to do on a holiday afternoon in Jinja? The answer is to go and see the Source of the Nile. Intrepid Victorian explorers argued long and hard over the location of the source of the White Nile. Armed with the obligatory copy of Bradt, we sit on a bench and read up on the story. John Henning Speke was the first European to see the great lake, which he named after the queen. He was convinced that the Nile flowed from Lake Victoria just outside Jinja, a theory hotly contested by Richard Burton who claimed the source was in Lake Tanganyika. A debate was arranged at the Royal Geographic Society, but hours before it was due to take place Speke went on a shooting expedition, tripped and shot himself. Several years later Sir Stanley Baker carried out a survey of Lake Victoria and pronounced that Speke was right.

Today the Source is a pleasant place for an afternoon visit with stalls lining the path selling souvenirs, cafes offering cold drinks and snacks and local dancing and singing groups providing entertainment. We queue up for a trip on the lake and once we have negotiated what is still probably an outrageous price, we clamber in and settle back to enjoy ourselves.

A few yards from land we are shown some ripples, which we are assured mark the genuine source of the White Nile, which will join the Blue Nile in Khartoum and eventually flow into the Mediterranean. Then the boat turns close to the rich vegetation of the banks. Perched high in the trees are the fish eagles, majestic with their black bodies, white heads and tail feathers. There are colonies of weaverbirds: tiny yellow birds, which live in large groups with the males competing to build the most elaborate nests to lure the females to mate with them. Being of an advanced age myself I quite like the idea of skill and experience triumphing over youth and enthusiasm and the weaverbird selection system certainly has my vote.

Stepping on to dry land we see the impressive monument to Gandhi, who in deference to the Hindu belief that ashes scattered on water enable the spirit to reach heaven quickly, instructed that his ashes be scattered on various rivers in the world including the Thames and the Nile. Some of his ashes were scattered in the river nearby and the Indian Government erected the memorial to mark the spot.

After our boat trip it is time for a cold drink and a rest in the shade before heading back to the town. The three of us have been invited to a concert where the entertainment consists of individuals going on stage to sing gospel songs or give testimonies about what Jesus means to them. A collection plate is passed round and the audience makes a donation according to the quality of the performance. It is lively and colourful and a world away from churches back home, but after an hour or so we agree we have overdosed on religion and slip away.

Work

My WATERPROOF WATCH has died, I've lost my glasses, my sandals have disappeared from outside my banda, my hair is orange from the dust and there are sightings of rats. One of the horror stories circulating about the latter is that they can scent meat in an unopened tin can. I'm assured they won't come near my hut as long as I don't keep food in it but I wonder if they have a taste for malaria pills.

Undeterred I'm up early for breakfast which is a lacklustre affair of tea, soggy white sliced bread and Blue Band margarine. The saving grace is my jar of Marmite brought from home, a present from a friend who told me mosquitoes hate the smell.

Then it's off to work. The project is being run from the Amagezi Education Centre in Kyabirwa. Built by SPE on land donated by the village, the centre holds daily sessions teaching life skills through drama, art, information technology, agriculture and science for P6 pupils, who are bused in from primary schools in the district. The emphasis is on participation and learning through fun and everyone enjoys a large lunch of beans, posho and motoki. The centre is also used for community activities: computer classes, agriculture and the occasional film show. This is to be our base, the place where the questionnaires will be sifted through and the report written.

Two American girls have arrived from Kenya and one is to work with me on the school leavers' project, while the other is to go up north to help assess the possibility of opening an SPE centre in Murchison National Park.

Katy is petite, dark and very beautiful. Jenny is bigger with red hair and a friendly face.

Katy talks a lot and Jenny listens. Katy's college fees are paid with a legacy from her grandmother, while Jenny paints houses in the vacation to cover hers.

I am working with Katy. Her degree is in experiential learning, and seems to consist of flying into foreign countries, working out their problems, keeping a diary and flying out again. It all sounds a lot more fun than struggling with Anglo Saxon and the great vowel shift.

We are briefed on the outline of the project. The age range of pupils in years six and seven is wide. Some who have attended school regularly from the age of six years will be twelve to thirteen. Others who started school late through lack of family funds, or who have had their education interrupted, may well be seventeen or eighteen.

While schools are well attended for the first four or five years, numbers drop off considerably towards the end of primary school and the aim of the project is to find out why this happens.

Twenty plus primary school head teachers have been contacted and told to expect a visit from an SPE volunteer. We are to go to each school, meet the heads, go through the questionnaires and leave them to be filled in. Returning the following week, we will then discuss the answers with each head teacher and collect the completed questionnaires.

Our boda drivers are ready and I clamber on, hoping mine has been picked for his caution, well serviced bike and accident free record.

I arrive at the first school, which is only about two miles away and wait for Katy. After ten minutes I start to worry that she is lying in the undergrowth.

Then they appear. Katy driving and Musa riding pillion with his arms clasped round her waist. Amid shrieks of laughter Katy tumbles off.

We walk along the path to the school office, passing small wooden signs very like the ones in stately homes requesting visitors to keep off the grass.

'Avoid under-age sex.'

'Keep yourself for marriage.'

'Do not take gifts in exchange for sex.'

Such notices form part of PIASCY the President's Initiative on AIDS Strategy for Communication to Youth, which hardly trips off the tongue, but has been effective. Uganda's speedy and energetic response to the problem attracted international acclaim. At its centre was ABC:

Abstain
Be faithful
Use a condom.

Sadly the US made support dependent on dropping the condom message. The policy also came under fire from some of the religious organisations that pour aid into Uganda. The campaign still continues but it is criticised for running out of steam as funding is diverted to different projects and the number of AIDS sufferers begins to climb.

We chat to the head who is grateful for the renovation work SPE has carried out at his school and is eager to help, assuring us that the completed questionnaire will be ready for collection in a few days. Back at the centre we talk over the schedule and realise that to cover all the schools we need to split up and tackle half each. Katy is to take the southern part of the sub-county nearest to Jinja town while I take the northern villages.

The next day it's Marmite for breakfast and off on the boda. I take care not to burn my leg on the exhaust and clutch my bottle of water over the bumps. We visit a couple of schools and then four or five miles from home my boda driver is out of his comfort zone. The map I have puzzles us both and I realise that my driver cannot read. Like many Ugandans who were in their teens when Universal Primary Education was introduced, he has never been to school. However he is happy to leap off his boda and enquire from locals the way to go and teachers at each school point us in the general direction of the next. With a few wrong turns we deliver our questionnaires.

In the evening I meet up with Katy. She has had a wonderful day. Musa took her out to lunch in Jinja. I point out that Musa is married with a baby, that the money he spent on Katy's lunch might have been needed to feed his family and by letting him treat her she may be giving him the wrong impression. It's none of my business and I should have kept quiet. To my own ears I sound like a Victorian housekeeper reprimanding a scullery maid for being too familiar with the gardener.

Katy is livid. 'I chose the cheapest meal on the menu and I am quite able to deal with the situation thank you.'

So that's me, quite rightly, put in my place.

The next day I arrive at the education centre to find the atmosphere stiff with tension.

Musa has declared undying love for Katy and told her she is his princess. Her reply that she is a freethinking independent twenty first century woman with no intention of being anyone's princess, has not gone down well. Katy goes off on my boda leaving me with a miserable Musa, trying to come to terms with the end of his dream life in the US with a beautiful muzungu.

My worry is that we need to get going and if Musa doesn't stop sulking, he is going to lose his job. Work on the SPE project means that for the next three or so weeks the two drivers receive a set daily wage instead of jostling at the boda station with a dozen or so others for whatever work comes their way. Musa is not irreplaceable and any one of the others would leap at the chance of his SPE work. He needs to sort his head out quickly. After what I hope sounds like light-hearted cajoling, I suggest we set off and after kicking a few more pebbles, Musa climbs on and starts the boda with a vicious jolt that almost has me in the bushes.

When we stop at our first school Musa mutters something under his breath and I realise that he thinks I am Katy's mother. I explain that I only met her three days ago and I am English and she is from the US. It falls on deaf ears. We look alike—well we are roughly the same colour and we are working together. It stands to reason that I am part of a dastardly muzungu plot to raise his hopes and then humiliate him. I am tempted to remind him that he has a partner and child and if he had got what he wanted they would have been left destitute. However I decide diplomacy is the way forward and try to calm ruffled feathers by offering him my spare bottle of water.

A few days later the questionnaires are all out and it's time to start collecting the first ones in.

Having been warned that the Ugandan time clock does not tick at the same rate as muzungu watches, I am prepared to go back to each school several times, but almost all heads have taken the matter seriously. Most of the questionnaires are ready for collection and the heads make time to talk through the results.

I arrive one morning at a Muslim school. The buildings are dirty and almost derelict by western standards. There seem to be no windows in some classrooms and those there are, are set so high in the wall that very little light filters in to brighten the gloom. It has been raining and the red mud is soft and treacherous beneath my feet, oozing up round my sandals and settling between my toes.

Outside the head's office I am met by a tall slim man wearing an immaculate white pin tucked and embroidered shirt reaching below his knees. The work in the garment is stunning and I find it hard to take my eyes off it and concentrate on its wearer.

'I'm from SPE I came last week and left a questionnaire with one of your staff who said it would be passed on to you.'

Mr Shirt shrugs. He doesn't have it.

"Please would you ask among your staff? It's important. We need it to carry out our research into school leavers.'

Mr Shirt is busy. He indicates the papers on his desk and shelves.

'Please would you try and find it.'

Feeling himself hedged into a corner by this pushy muzungu woman, Mr Shirt points to a chair and disappears into the room next door.

He is gone only a few minutes but looks vastly relieved on his return.

'I have made enquiries. The papers are in the cupboard.'

'Great, please may I have them?'

Like a conjuror pulling a rabbit out of a hat he delivers his lines with a flourish.

'The cupboard is locked. The man with the keys has gone home.'

'Does he live close by?'

'No no and he is ill.'

'If I go to my next school and return in a couple of hours, could you have the papers ready for me? Otherwise I shall have to make another journey and that will be expensive and waste money that could be spent on a school such as yours.'

Aware that he has some sort of let-out and his face can be saved, Mr Shirt strokes his beautiful cuffs and agrees that if I return in a couple of hours but not before, all will be well.

On my return to the education centre with the questionnaire, I tell the others about my interview.

Apparently the keys to the cupboard ploy is well worn in Uganda, to the point where Dr Ian Clarke who founded a mission hospital in Kiwoko, Central Uganda in the 1980s called his memoirs *The Man with the Key Has Gone.*

Findings

*T*HE COMPLETED QUESTIONNAIRES are in front of us and we have a fortnight to analyse them and write a report to be used in funding applications by SPE. There are twenty two returns. Information includes the number of children registered, national exam results, difficulties faced by pupils in attending school and reasons why there is such a heavy drop-out rate in years six and seven. Further sections examine the languages in which lessons are taught and ways in which the SPE Amagezi Education Centre can further assist the local community.

Although the introduction of free primary education was a huge step forward, schooling is still out of reach for many. It applies only to the first four children in a family and Ugandan families are large. Parents have to buy a uniform for each child. This consists of dresses for girls and shirts for boys, usually made from stiff man-made fabric and always in eye blinking colours: fuchsia pink and canary yellow being prime favourites. Stationery in the form of exercise books and pencils needs to be purchased and in some cases, a school fee is charged. For many education still remains a dream.

Schools filling in the questionnaire have been asked their feelings about the language used for lessons in the education centre. There are thirty three languages spoken in Uganda, so there is little chance that English will ever be replaced as the official one. In the Jinja area children speak Luganda or Lusogo. It is not until they arrive at school that they start to learn English. After three years all lessons are delivered in English in preparation for public exams. Replies from schools reflect nervousness at being seen to be failing to deal with language issues. Some admit that pupils find it difficult to follow lessons in English. Findings show the centre needs to continue giving local language support while carrying out activities in English.

Collecting data about pupils' movements is not an easy business. Pupils may miss a term or even a year's lessons while parents try to scrape together the necessary money. Death or illness of a relative can mean a move to a new area as families regroup. All the schools make a brave attempt at providing figures, but in some cases these are based on wishful thinking rather than concrete facts. Around half of the figures provided are thought to be reasonably accurate. Of the others one school has more pupils passing national exams than are registered and several boast a hundred per cent pass rate over four years. Eager to be seen as a positive learning environment some claim an annual attendance rate in the high nineties.

The main reasons for pupils dropping out of school are ill health and poverty. Life is tough for rural families and children have to pull their weight. A Ugandan colleague confirms the findings with his own childhood experience. Woken at around six in the morning he would go out to the family plot for gardening. After a couple of hours the family would return home to eat any food remaining from the night before. Often there was nothing and he would head off for school on an empty stomach. At lunchtime he walked home to fill jerry cans at the standpipe. In all probability there would still be no food in the house. After school it was more gardening and at last a meal before sleep.

According to the material in the questionnaire, his story is a common one. Pupils walk long distances to school usually on an empty stomach. All the schools say the majority of pupils go without a midday meal. In one where a lunch of porridge is provided for around seventy pence a term only two hundred pupils out of nine hundred take the meal. Hunger leaves pupils exhausted and unable to concentrate.

Hunger also brings vulnerability to disease. Malaria is a major problem. The Ugandan Government runs a net programme and Soft Power Health a sister organisation of SPE does runs distributing nets, selling them at a minimal cost, demonstrating their use and giving advice on who should sleep under them. Parents may sleep under the nets themselves reasoning that they need to stay healthy in order to look after their children. However malaria is the biggest killer of children under five years and the most common cause of miscarriage, so it is young children and pregnant women who most need to sleep under the nets. Using the nets properly is not easy. They need to be suspended from the roof and to be tucked firmly under a mattress. In many homes there is nowhere from which to hang the nets and children frequently sleep on a blanket or rug on the floor.

Anti-malarial drugs are available at pharmacies and clinics but the costs represent a huge hole in a weekly budget. Families may have to delay seeking medical help for a very sick child until they have scraped together the five thousand shillings or so necessary for medicine. Visitors staying for less than six months take a prophylactic to ward off malaria. Long term residents have to take their chance. However while malaria is no respecter of persons, healthy muzungus able to seek immediate treatment, usually make a full recovery from the flulike symptoms. The effect on local people can be much more serious.

Despite the government campaign AIDS is a massive scourge. Seen as shameful, it is not a subject for open discussion and those at risk often delay being tested for as long as they feel reasonably well, hoping for the best and infecting other people. Orphans in Uganda are children who have lost one parent, not necessarily both. When one parent is HIV positive, the chances are the other one will also be infected. The burden of care then falls on the extended family, which has little choice but to take in the offspring. One head teacher put the number of orphans in his school at fifty per cent Several schools mention that frequent deaths within a family lead to absence from lessons as children accompany their parents to funerals.

Stomach upsets caused by unclean water or contaminated food are problems listed by many schools, so is bilharzia, caught from washing, swimming or playing in local lakes and rivers. Two schools list snake bites as a concern because children who cannot afford school meals go off to play in the woods in their bare feet during the lunch break. Measles is still on the list but the number of cases has dropped considerably thanks to a national inoculation programme.

Worms, eye infections, diabetes, yellow fever, asthma, sickle cell anaemia, yams (a local name for a sexually transmitted disease): the list is long and the afternoon is hot. Distracted, I key in the words, as I would a shopping list for Sainsbury's. Then come back, ashamed, to a catalogue of human suffering I can scarcely comprehend from my cossetted western background.

Teenage pregnancy is common, but often difficult to pinpoint as girls leave school before their condition becomes obvious. Cross-generational sex is a major problem in Uganda and staff at one school are concerned that some girls are sleeping with older men in exchange for school uniforms and equipment. The issue is being addressed with a government campaign. Along the road to Kampala are posters of a lecherous middle-aged man making eyes at a young girl. The words below read:

'Would you like this man to sleep with your daughter?'

Twenty yards on a second poster reads:

'Then why are you sleeping with his?'

'Defilement'—having sex with a child under eighteen is a serious offence, but still the level of sexual abuse and rape is high. For many victims legal redress is out of reach and a family just has to accept that there is another mouth to feed. Girls settle into relationships and have children while still young. Few can afford legal marriage eremonies and opt for common law relationships hoping that they will last. Many have little choice in the matter, while others possibly see a relationship as an escape from the drudgery of family life.

In the words of one teacher:

'Few girls can afford secondary education so marriage is one of very few options.'

Ironically given the high incidence of teenage pregnancies, Ugandans are modest and reluctant to talk about personal matters. Public shows of affection between couples are rare. Hanging pants and bras out to dry where they can be seen by passers-by is frowned upon, which means my shower is festooned with underwear most of the time.

Girls who are lucky enough to have an uninterrupted education face difficulties during menstruation. Unable to afford sanitary protection, they have to stay at home during their periods and miss valuable lessons. Hygiene lessons for boys and girls at Amagezi include making sanitary protection out of clean rags folded over a polythene pad.

Around ten per cent of families are Moslem, but it is not only Moslem men who take more than one wife. Long established tribal traditions mean that many Christian families include several wives. Offspring are a sign of virility and when a wife ceases to bear children she can be retired and a younger model brought in.

One friend married to a Ugandan had a visit from her parents who were invited by her father-in law to meet the rest of the family. Her father is still recovering from being introduced to seven mamas and over fifty children. The downside of such arrangements is that so many people are dependent on one man who cannot afford to feed or educate them properly.

When a mother dies the father is likely to remarry quickly and stepmothers are regarded with suspicion. As one teacher said:

'When a stepmother cooks it is her own children who are fed.'

Once a child reaches an age when he or she can be useful, they must take their share of responsibility for the family. Boys earn money sugar cane cutting, brick making or stone quarrying, while girls look after younger children or sick relatives.

Teachers have their own problems to face. Pay in government schools is not high and often erratic. It is difficult to engage children with classes so large and equipment so sparse. The universal 'I blame the parents' appears regularly in the questionnaires. Drunkenness and drug taking are mentioned as reasons why parents do not take their responsibilities seriously. Lax parenting means children neglect their studies, play truant and drift into bad company.

One school mentions negative peer pressure as a very serious problem because pupils are encouraged to skip school to watch DVDs at a trading centre where a local entrepreneur has rigged up an ingenious system run on car batteries.

Smoking dope is an issue although rightly or wrongly this seems to be regarded as affecting boys rather than girls. The boys then allegedly become less sexually inhibited and lead the girls astray.

Most parents do take their children's education seriously. One family, delighted a son had sponsorship for secondary education was dismayed when they learnt on the grapevine that he was truanting in order to hang around the river with the kayakers.

His older brother read him the riot act and the boy insisted the rumours were untrue. He was then ordered to bring his schoolbooks home so his brother could check his progress. The books appeared covered in newspaper and every subject was up to date. On close examination the writing in every one was different and removal of the covers showed the books belonged to various friends.

However committed a family might be to educating their children, the findings of the report show the massive problems faced by local communities.

Most people are subsistence farmers growing food to feed their families and hoping to have something left over to sell. For some women the struggle to make extra money, ends in a drinking spree for husbands. Whatever the domestic situation poor farming methods mean low yields. There are few local markets and no good road systems. Landowners who hit hard times sell pieces of land to bring in money and then have even less land from which to make a living.

Response to the section asking for ideas in which SPE can support local communities reflects an intense desire for a better quality of life. Adult literacy levels are low and basic literacy classes are high on the list of requests as is the installation of boreholes and water tanks to improve water supplies. Other suggestions are advice on crop diversification, subsidised tools and seeds, poultry and pig units and the introduction of bee keeping on a commercial basis.

Several villages request further net trips from Soft Power Health and the return of the popular family planning visits. Despite Ugandan modesty these provide entertainment for the whole village. From four years to eighty they all gather to hear about the Pill-Plan, the Inject-a-Plan and to roll around with laughter at the sight of a muzungu fitting a condom on a banana. With luck the visits result in a few more clinic appointments and increased uptake of the condoms left in a covered box nailed to the wall of the SPH clinic.

Together Katy and I struggle to bring the findings together into a readable report that will be useful to SPE in considering future activities and applying for funding. We have settled into a working relationship and are rubbing along together, so I tell myself, as I press the final 'save' button on my section of the work.

'Finished' I say with an air of satisfaction.

'Send it to me' is Katy's reply. 'I need to check your spelling and punctuation.'

Murchison

I'VE GIVEN UP on the soggy bread and margarine and have started having breakfast at De Nile Cafe, next door to the campsite. I can't resist the invitation on the wall:

'Relax in stylee in De Nilee.'

Plus they do a good sausage sandwich and a great cup of tea.

Last week Eithne and Loretta went off to Murchison Falls on safari. I felt I couldn't go away until the report was finished so I was delighted when Malin, a Swedish volunteer suggested we team up for a trip. Murchison is top of the list for most tourists. Situated in the north west of Uganda, it is the largest park in the country. Despite the mayhem of the Amin years, civil war and poaching, it is home to over seventy mammal species including growing numbers of lions, plus elephants, hippos and giraffes

Early Friday morning and we're all ready for a great weekend. At eight o clock there is a delay because the truck's battery is flat. We retire for another sausage sandwich and set out an hour late for a hunt round Jinja for diesel. Fuel comes from Kenya and there is a national shortage, so the search takes some time. Finally seven of us plus cook, driver and guide move north.

Working long hours on the report I have not investigated the trip in any detail.

I did speak to Eithne and Loretta about their jaunt, which I assumed would be similar to mine. Theirs, they said was great—lots to see, static tents with proper beds, loos, showers, restaurants. Mine has to be better as it costs more and includes an extra day.

First stop is a supermarket in a shopping precinct in Kampala. It's just like home: air conditioning, packets of sliced ham, bottles of wine, disposable nappies and loads of muzungus pushing trolleys. It's only when you leave that you notice the armed guards keeping undesirables (locals with no money) out. Our guide tells us this is our last contact with civilisation so we need to buy anything we can't do without for the next three days. Overwhelmed by the gravity of the situation I wander round the aisles and leave with a packet of ginger biscuits.

After a couple of hours in the truck Emma, one of the passengers, complains of feeling unwell and has come out in a rash. There is a debate about what to do and Emma insists we carry on. I feel concerned that her reply is based on not spoiling the trip for the rest of us. I notice Emma's head shaking violently and fear she is having a fit. I then notice other passengers bobbing up and down as we bump over rocky unsurfaced roads.

In around three hours we make it to the Ziwa Rhino Sanctuary and receive a stern talk from a park ranger.

'Rhinos are dangerous when they charge. Do not run. They can run faster than you. Do as I say. If I say climb tree, climb. Rhinos know me. They like my smell. To them you are strange.'

My chances of climbing a ladder let alone a tree are minimal, so I decide hanging around the back of the group is probably my best option.

The rhino population in Uganda has been virtually destroyed by poaching and numbers in the rest of sub-Saharan Africa have been drastically diminished. Thanks to myths around the power of rhino horn, the value of the average horn has risen to around three hundred and forty thousand dollars. It is seen as powerful medicine, a cure for cancer and an aphrodisiac, much sought after across China, Vietnam and Indonesia. In reality horns are made from keratin, the same material as finger nails, so if the stories were in any way true, people who bite their nails would have a great life and live forever.

Today rhinos are hunted by poachers working for wealthy international syndicates, using helicopters, night vision equipment, high calibre weapons and veterinary drugs. Both black and white rhinos are actually grey, but the white ones are slightly bigger. In 1970 there were an estimated three hundred black rhinos in Uganda and one hundred and twenty white rhinos. By the early 1980s they had both been poached to extinction. Today the only rhinos in the country are the six in the sanctuary of which two came from Kenya and four from Disney Animal Kingdom in the US. They are well protected within the sanctuary by a solar powered electric fence because given half a chance the poachers would be in there.

The visit grows more bizarre as we learn the rhinos' names. Only one, Bella, takes any interest in us. She gives us one sweeping look and then when the park ranger says 'Bella be calm' she wanders off looking bored.

Back at the truck we find it has sunk into a swamp and it takes an hour and a half to get it out. We drive for two hours in the rain and the dark to our first campsite, which looks suspiciously like a car park adjoining a hotel with an iron palisade around it. There is an armed guard and a Japanese coach parked next to us.

I hear the guide ask if we mind sharing tents as it is wet and getting late! A friendly Australian called Lyn offers to be my tent mate which is gratifying as I don't want to feel like the last one picked for the form rounders team.

We are given a tent and told to put it up. I try to make myself useful as the thought of static beds begins to fade. I have brought a sleeping bag but no mattress, so the guide lends me his spare. It must have belonged to his pet cat because it is only about three feet long. Still beggars can't be choosers. Once the tent is up and while the cook finds the pans, Lyn and I slope off to the hotel for a gin and tonic.

In the morning I see the first of many interesting sights: the Japanese coach loading up, with a man in the back seat adjusting his neighbour's oxygen mask while smoking a cigarette. As we stand around the back of the truck drinking tea, Lyn regales our fellow travellers with the news that she thought she was sleeping with the Queen Mother because I actually put on pyjamas before climbing into my sleeping bag.

We're off to Budongo Forest to trek chimpanzees. The animals are in their natural habitat but are habituated to humans, so they have grown accustomed to them and take little notice of visitors. The argument is that this is the only way to observe animals in forest settings, but the more I think about habituation the less comfortable I am.

In the early days the process centred on putting food out which weakened the animals' ability to find their own food. Today this is frowned upon, but there are still issues about making wild animals comfortable with humans. We don't have a very good track record when it comes to concern for other species and tourists and hunters must look much the same to a chimp. Proximity to man brings disease and danger. While it might be enjoyable for us, I can't help feeling the chimps could be the losers.

After three hours trekking we come across a large family group up in the trees and settle down to watch them. One poor female chimp is on heat and is pestered every five minutes or so by what the guide euphemistically calls 'her boyfriends'. During the time when a female is fertile she is mounted by most males in the group, which means that the whole group feels responsibility for the babies and the gene pool is extended.

Back in the coach Emma has a high temperature and a livid rash. Her friend Jen is feeling unwell and also showing signs of a rash. We park at a campsite near the river crossing, and the guide takes both girls to a medical centre about an hour away.

They return with medication and the news that Emma and Jen have been bitten by insects and their rashes are an allergic reaction. A couple of days ago Emma went swimming and left her towel on the grass. The likelihood is that she was bitten as she dried herself. This would also explain Jen's problem as the self same towel was hanging over the seat she and Emma were sharing on the truck.

Despite being unwell Emma insists she is fine to continue and we load up on the truck only to discover it has broken down yet again. Treacherously my hopes turn to the static tents and beds close by, but two hours later we are on the ferry and crossing into Murchison. Half submerged in the water relaxing in the shade of the banks are numerous hippos. With their huge bodies they look unlikely ever to make a move, but when threatened they can become very aggressive. At night they come out of the water to munch huge quantities of grass and are capable of outrunning a human being.

Back on the truck we travel through grassland and scrub broken by occasional clusters of acacia and baobab trees. Only the animals are missing. Like the hippos they are snoozing through the hot African afternoon. We make camp a couple of hours into the park in the Nile Delta, close to the river, with a stunning view across to the Democratic Republic of Congo. The animals may not be visible but as darkness falls we can hear them wandering around outside our tents. An armed park ranger guards our camp through the night, protecting us from the animals and them from us.

It's a short night and before dawn we slip away in the truck to see lions, rhinos, giraffes, antelope, wart hogs, baboons and crocodiles. While no other animal in Uganda has suffered as much as the rhino, many face problems even in a national park. Elephants are in danger from ivory hunters and numbers are down from around thirty thousand in the 1960s to four thousand. The number of lions has dropped by around sixty per cent in ten years and while Uganda is reputedly the best place in the world for giraffes, the Ugandan or Rothschild giraffe is down to around two hundred and fifty.

The most difficult animal to see, has to be the leopard and we didn't manage it. These beautiful solitary creatures are well camouflaged and so hard to spot. The main threat to them is the loss of habitat as land is taken for agriculture. All the animals are in danger from bush meat traps set by local people for whom the cost of other meats has become too high. The most common trap is made of wire extended between trees.

Never having thought of myself as an animal person I am unprepared for the sheer delight of watching wild creatures in their natural habitat, their colours so vibrant and their movement so elegant. The loss of such animals would be appalling and clearly there is a need to protect them. Yet if I were a hungry local with no money and a family to feed. I know what I would do.

Lost for words we head back for breakfast and then pack away our tents.

In the afternoon we take a boat trip to the spectacular Murchison Falls where the Nile is forced through a twenty three feet gap in the rocks and then cascades down a hundred and forty feet drop before flowing westwards into Lake Albert. Named Murchison Falls by Sir Stanley Baker after the then president of the Royal Geographic Society, the falls were renamed Kabarega Falls for a short time by Idi Amin. Exhausted by the early morning start, the heat and the gentle movement of the boat, I fall asleep and to my shame have to be nudged awake to disembark and clamber up the path to the top of the falls.

A great weekend and thanks to Lyn I can now put up a tent.

Unwelcome Visitors

*H*EATHROW AIRPORT IS humming with Christmas cheer and dripping with tinsel and I am delighted to be leaving it all behind. A festive email has gone out saying I am making a donation to SPE this year in lieu of cards and now I am off. This time my trip is for two whole months and for the first three weeks I shall be house-sitting about three miles outside Bujagali with Eithne. As a concession to the festive season my younger son Julian and his partner Anna will be coming out for a week.

The house is built on the banks of the Nile at the end of a long dirt track. The family is busy packing, hunting for warm clothes that haven't seen the light of day since their last trip home. Still they find time to give me a rudimentary driving lesson in the Nissan Safari. Then it's suggested I drive up to the village and collect Eithne. I had hoped for more 'getting to know you' time, but gingerly turn the ignition key and jolt up the track.

I thought I made quite a good fist of it, but later I hear from Cibbi that the local joke was that just about everybody in the village could walk faster than I was driving.

Disconcertingly the fuel gauge seems to be permanently on empty so we decide it is probably broken and we don't need to bother too much about it. Eventually Julian will point out that it is on empty because the tank contains virtually no fuel and our miserly couple of gallons every few days are having no effect on the fuel gauge.

We wave goodbye to our friends and left to our own devices Eithne and I mooch around the empty house, unpacking and making cups of tea. By six o'clock the isolation is affecting us both and we decide to drive into Bujagali to say hello to whoever might be there.

Eithne has conveniently left her driving licence safely in Tipperary so I am permanent chauffeur. Feeling like an old hand I make it up the hill to the village and we settle down with a coke each to watch the world go by.

Night comes quickly in Uganda. It is light and then in ten minutes it is dark. Too late I realise day has slipped away. With no lights from lamps or windows, I have to find our way home. We make it to the wider busier road with a sigh of relief. The only remaining obstacle is recognising the point at which we turn off down the track.

'It's just past the football pitch next to a house painted half blue and half brown'.

The night is so dark we can't see the houses let alone their colour. I overshoot the track twice and turning is a nightmare. Eventually I find it and off we go at around two miles an hour negotiating rocks and potholes and branches of trees.

The house looms out of the darkness and having got us there I luxuriate in relief and the thought that nothing will ever worry me again.

Standing in front of the house are three men. One is wearing a floor length hooded cloak and resembles the Grim Reaper. The others are Milton who looks after the garden and Moses the ascari or night watchman. The Grim Reaper is Moses' friend.

They have gathered together to await our return and to inform us one of the family dogs has been killed. The body is lying in front of us. It is Sushi much loved by the children who have known her all their lives. A few weeks ago she had two puppies, which were with her in the house.

It must be our fault. We must have let her out. How did she die? Did I hit her as I drove away? Eithne reassures me that at the speed I drive I could not have delivered a fatal blow to a grass hopper.

The guys are excited. They are key players in one of the most thrilling events for a long time. They say they know who did the deed and will take us to the home of the boy they are sure has killed the dog and he will be beaten. On further questioning it becomes clear that nobody actually saw anything and so much to the disappointment of the trio we turn down the chance of a march through the village and a public flogging.

The phone number for the vet is on the fridge and I ring and beg him to come over. He says it will cost around ten pounds and I say that is fine. He arrives half an hour later, tells us the dog is dead and asks for his money. Pressed further he examines the dog and says she died from a blow on the head.

Taking comfort from the phone I try to ring the family to tell them their pet has died. Then stricken with panic about what to do with the remains, I ring a friend in the UK who suggests putting the body in the freezer. It would get it out the way but what to do with the food that's already in there? Plus there are power cuts every day, so defrosting could be an issue.

I'm like I was in labour—glued to the gas and air machine although it did no good at all. I dial another friend and tell the story once again. Bury the dog, is the answer. Ask the men to dig a deep hole in a shady part of the garden under a bush or a tree and bury her. Shaking with shock I persuade Eithne to open the bottle of Baileys she has brought over for Christmas and we indulge in a long conversation in which I maintain my guilt and she assures me I do not have blood on my hands.

The two puppies appear not to miss their mother too much. They were fully weaned before her death but were being kept in the house because of the risk of birds of prey swooping down and carrying them off for supper. They are lively and fun and manage to climb, pee and poo everywhere. The first job every morning is to clear up after them.

Household pets include a mangy parrot, which has pulled out all its body feathers because it is in mourning for its original family and doesn't like women. A hamster, probably sensing our record with living creatures, took to its bedding on our arrival. Fearing a second burial could be in the offing, there is great relief when one evening there is a faint sound of rustling from its cage.

We get to know our neighbours who seem pleasant and friendly and not dog clubbing types at all. Milton the handyman who lives on the property hates Moses the night watchman and tells me in confidence at least twice a day that Moses killed the dog! Moses arrives once it is dark usually accompanied by the Grim Reaper who knocks on the door and scares us stiff.

Stella comes in daily to wash and clean, bringing with her Tarvine her son, who is three years old and deaf. The level of deafness among children in the area seems very high by UK standards. Possibly because without medical treatment, which most people cannot afford, it is impossible to know whether a condition is untreatable or simply a case of glue ear or even impacted wax.

Stella and Tarvine live in a tiny brick room. She is lively and friendly and seems to be making the most of her tough existence. Her family live in the village and she and her son go to see them every weekend, but the rest of the time she is on her own.

The Ugandan Christmas holidays are around two months long with schools breaking up at the end of November and returning at the end of January. Still there is work to be done and one job with which we are entrusted is to take some cash to Felix the village councillor or LC1 for the purchase of a field. It is to be used by the agricultural group set up by SPE to test the cultivation of new crops and the introduction of sustainable farming methods. Fred who works at the education centre as a gardener, is to prepare the ground for planting early in the New Year.

Eithne and I deliver the money to Felix. By local standards he is well off and wields a fair amount of power. He owns quite a lot of land around the village while his wife and daughter have a stall selling local crafts. Felix is the only person I have met in Bujagali who wears spectacles.

He counts the money and declares himself to be satisfied. A couple of days later we meet Fred who tells us he can't prepare the land because there is a crop of tomato plants growing on it!

Off we go to see Felix who says he has let a guy dig the field but is shocked to hear he has planted a crop, suggesting the digging had been purely for fun. Sensing our scepticism Felix tells us the guy is landless and penniless and needs compensation for his crop. We suggest Felix should pay him compensation not SPE at which point Felix announces the field isn't his and he is selling it on behalf of an old woman. Then Fred, Eithne and I are taken on a sightseeing trip to view the field, which is about twenty yards along the road but a good ten minutes walk via the scenic route. We end the meeting sweaty and disorientated and tell Felix we have no money or power to make any decision but will report back to the people who have.

We return to the field a few days later with Cibbi who negotiates a settlement whereby some of the plants remain until after the harvest! I decline the offer of another trip to view the field, feeling it can't have changed dramatically in a week.

Julian and Anna arrive a couple of days before Christmas. They go quad biking. Julian goes white water rafting and the three of us go horse riding. Not having been on a horse since I was fifteen, I manage quite well, especially the first part, sitting watching the world go by. Rising to the trot is more difficult and after two hours in the saddle I can scarcely dismount let alone stand upright.

The day before Christmas Eve we return home to find the kitchen table laden with food and bottles of wine. Puzzled we stack the goodies away and take guesses as to the identity of our fairy godmother.

On Christmas Eve we go into the village and are discussing the possibility of a chilled out evening when we are approached by a group of four kayakers and one girlfriend.

Are we going back to the house? Great they'll come with us. Yes they are here for Christmas. The owner said if they were around Jinja at Christmas they were welcome to stay in the house and here they are. They dropped by yesterday with their provisions but nobody was in.

What follows is festive parallel house sharing. Attempts at conversation and offers of joint meals are met with complete surprise. They are happy watching videos and unfazed by our presence. They have no wish to engage with us and assume we feel the same about them.

Eithne mentions Christmas Day. As we are in the same house might it be pleasant to eat together? They are not sure. They are planning a late breakfast and more videos.

Christmas morning the parallel group sleep in and we go to mass with Eithne, at least I do. Julian and Anna can't get in for the crush. The singing is beautiful. The sermon is long and confusing. It seems to have a lot to do with witchcraft and threats from the priest to carry out spot checks on the children to see if they are wearing charms to ward off evil spirits. I vow to give up witchcraft, burn my broomstick and hat and throw away my cauldron and book of spells.

On our return video watching is in full swing and the sink is full of breakfast dishes. The mention of lunch in a couple of hours elicits a mumble or two and we settle down to make salads.

Whatever else is on the table, it's not good cheer. By nine o'clock we have done the washing up and retired to bed with Eithne declaring it has been the worst Christmas of her life, that she is mad with homesickness for Tipperary and will never leave Ireland in December ever again.

On Boxing Day we get up to find a note saying the parallel party has found the scene too quiet and headed off in search of something livelier. They don't know if they will be coming back. Relieved that peace on earth and good will towards men is over for another year, we give up on the festivities with a sigh of relief.

Julian has a meeting with Ernest the SPE science teacher, so we head for the education centre. Anna and I wander over to the Soft Power Health centre and chat to a volunteer who tells us members of staff are examining a very sick child. Five minutes later a nurse comes out to say the girl aged around twelve needs to go to hospital in Jinja. The patient is the granddaughter of Mama Joyce who runs a restaurant in the village. Mama Joyce has summoned a bicycle and she and the driver are trying to tie the girl who is screaming with pain, onto the saddle.

We offer a lift and what follows is a nightmare journey with Prossy the girl wimpering and screaming every time we go over a bump. We arrive at the first hospital to be told it only takes patients over thirteen years so we have to cross town to the children's hospital. A couple of days later Mama Joyce sees us to thank us for the lift and tells us Prossy has been taken to Kampala for tests.

Kenya is a hot topic of conversation because of unrest and violence erupting over elections. The borders are closed and fuel prices are soaring. Trouble in Kenya immediately affects Uganda as imported goods come in via Kenyan ports. It's also worrying that a country, which was considered stable by African standards looks to be dissolving into chaos.

The holiday ends. Our visitors leave and Eithne and I return to work. One of our jobs is to welcome volunteers and to make sure their stay runs smoothly. A Canadian couple arrive and we arrange to meet them early in the evening. Returning home we find that the side gate of the garden is open and the dogs are out.

We get them back in by waving pieces of meat over the netting. They all seem fine and we try to think no more about it. The house boasts a proper bath and I am having a hot soak and reading a good book when I hear Eithne talking heatedly to someone outside the window.

In the drive are the local village chairman and a farmer carrying a washing up bowl in which lies a very dead, skinned and jointed goat. All that is needed is Jamie Oliver and a sprig of parsley. Allegedly the dogs have killed the goat although in the state it is in it is hard to tell what caused its demise—dogs' teeth or butcher's knife.

The chairman demands money as compensation and suggests we might like to eat the goat. I decline the offer as I am not keen on munching a carcase with such a chequered history.

The next suggestion is that we buy the remains of the goat for the dogs as they clearly enjoy the flavour.

I am tempted to pay the asking price for an easy life. Then I catch sight of Eithne who sensing my weakness is shaking her head vigorously. She is right. We have most likely been set up. Is it just coincidence that within a day of being on our own another incident has occurred? If I pay the goat ransom what will happen next?

Somebody is viewing the muzungu women as an easy target and we need to make a stand. Firmly we insist that the owners of the house and the dogs will be back in less than a week and any complaints about the incident must be made to them. The farmer and the chairman are not happy, but eventually leave. True to form Moses tells us Milton let the dogs out and Milton is certain it was Moses.

Then there is an attempt to blame Stella who, like many Ugandans is terrified of dogs. The final straw comes with the suggestion that Tarvine who at three years old and at least a foot short of the bolt on the gate, is the culprit.

With relief we welcome the family back and move up to bandas on the Eden Rock campsite where my only concern is keeping tabs on my Marmite.

No local ever mentioned the matter of the dogs and the goat to the family.

Buwidgee

*T*HE CHRISTMAS SERMON is still lingering in my mind. I am increasingly fascinated by the idea of witchcraft.

Black magic exists here side by side with Christianity and Islam. I am yet to see a baby who doesn't sport a red woven thread around its middle or wrist for protection against evil spirits and at the end of the village surrounded by a wooden palisade lives the local witch doctor, known as the Bujagali, apparently famous throughout Uganda. According to local belief the Bujagali is a river spirit who over the centuries has manifested itself into a series of men with magical powers. To prove the possession of such supernatural gifts each contender is required to float across the rapids in the Nile on a piece of barkcloth.

Last week the head teacher of one of the local secondary schools was discovered by his staff, burying a goat's head in the playground to ensure he kept his job for life. The staff, none too pleased, went on strike and all the pupils were sent home.

My interest has been fuelled by a chat with Romeo. He has been to university in Kampala and is back in Jinja hunting for a job. It is not easy for graduates to find work and he is under pressure from his family who sold precious land to finance his degree studies and now need him to fund the education of his younger brothers and sisters.

Romeo explained why Ugandans have large families and listed the diseases that reduce life expectancy to the late forties. He mentions malaria and HIV and then says buwidgee is very serious. I reply that I have never heard of it and ask him to spell the word out. On his hand he traces the word 'bewitching'.

Many people die from bewitching. If there is someone who is getting on your nerves or if you want something badly, like a great deal of money, you go along to the local witch doctor and he sees you alright. The downside is you give him a goat or two and then the next week he wants a couple more, then it's a cow, then the head of your favourite wife or the body of your first born, so it can become quite heavy.

The reason for the witch doctor's demands is that he has to appease the ghosts, which live around the Nile and are hungry and difficult to satisfy. There are many ghosts because so many bodies have been thrown into the river over the years. They take many forms—a flash of lightning, a white cloud, a wisp of smoke. If you see one you will soon die so best walk around with your eyes closed.

Romeo knows of a girl who was possessed by demons, which kept telling her to leave school. Her parents spent a fortune taking her to witch doctors but the spirits were too strong. In the end they took her to a fundamentalist church in Kampala where the minister was well known for his powers. It took five relatives to drag her into church and sit on her because the spirits were so angry. After several visits the spirits were defeated. Interestingly she never went back to school.

Intrigued I talk the matter over with Cibbi who loses no time in pointing out how ridiculous it all is.

'Do you really think that if the fellow at the end of the road had power over life and death he would be living in a mud hut in Buj? He feeds on ignorance and fear and talks complete nonsense. I don't challenge his ideas openly because it would make my life difficult. My chickens might be killed, my washing stolen, the tyres of my bike punctured. But that is the level of his power.'

Of course he is right. However the stories of bewitching remain disconcerting. A muzungu woman, well settled in the area for many years, told me how upset she was over the death of a kayaker's mother. The woman had suffered from a stomach tumour for nine years, which began to grow at an alarming rate. Eventually a volunteer offered to pay for her to go into a clinic and have it investigated. The news was good. The tumour was benign. The patient was recovering well and enjoying a spot of luxury in her private room, including playing with the remote control for the television. The day she was due to be discharged she received a message from her son saying he could not pick her up and she was to stay an extra night. The next morning she was dead. Everyone was at a loss to know why she died, but at her funeral a woman came forward picked up a clod of earth, dropped it on the coffin and announced 'This is my power'!

The village is alive with such stories, which can linger for years, gaining potency as time goes by. The father of a family took a second wife when his first wife had one son and was pregnant with her second child. According to her children the first wife was unhappy and upset about the matter but accepted it, thankful that her husband was able to build on another bedroom and the trio did not have to share. Several years passed and the women managed to live their lives in an amicable fashion. One day the first wife swallowed a fish bone, which stuck in her throat and she choked to death. That was over twenty years ago, but her family still blame the second wife for having cursed her and caused her end.

It's all very confusing and the more I try to put it out of my mind the more it pops back. I walk past the Bujagali's property and notice he now has a car—not the newest model, but definitely a car. I make a mental note to tell Cibbi.

Life is becoming interesting here as the school term approaches. I attend an enrolment day for one of the two SPE pre-schools. First places go to AIDS orphans and the room is full of women, children and babies. Many of the former look tired and careworn and are clearly grandmothers or great-aunts. An hour after we are due to start the teacher phones to say there has been a death in her family. Romeo, there to represent his father who is on the committee and Florence the cleaner, decide to get started. The crowd quietens as Romeo announces that names, ages of children and their circumstances will be written down and aferwards a decision made about who is to be given a place. Are there any questions?

A voice from the back asks 'When will Soft Power Education open the new primary school in the village'?

Romeo translates for me but I don't understand him. He turns back to the speaker, whose question has been taken up enthusiastically by others. The nearest primary school is in the neighbouring village, but parents feel it is overcrowded. SPE has done a lot to help the village and a school is the next step.

The light begins to dawn and I try to set the matter right. 'I am here for the enrolment and to report back on the number of children seeking places. SPE doesn't build and fund schools. It works with the government to repair and renovate those that exist already.'

Heads shake in disbelief. The presence of a muzungu at the meeting has raised hopes and a rumour has quickly spread that the hoped for school is to become a reality.

Don't I see the need for a school in the village?

I could do something if I chose.

Through Romeo I repeat that I am just a volunteer and have no say at all in decisions made by SPE. Eyes are averted, people are too polite to argue, but their disappointment is palpable. I could help them if I wanted and have decided not to do so.

SPE has gained respect locally as an organisation that delivers on its promises and has made a positive difference to schooling in the area, but funds are finite and needs great.

On the eastern outskirts of Jinja is an area poor by local standards where very few people own their own land. Many of them are Karamajong who have moved down from the north east of Uganda, where they were cattle rearers on poor drought prone land. Karamajong are regarded by their countrymen as primitive and backward with a habit of going naked. Their homeland borders on Kenya and cattle raids both ways across the border are commonplace. As their traditional way of life is eroded Karamajong are moving away from tribal lands to other parts of Uganda, but often find it difficult to gain acceptance.

The primary school in the area inhabited by the newcomers, is supported by several international organisations to provide education and food for children. The aim is to try and keep them in school rather than have them drifting on to the streets. Unfortunately the children, less than keen on full-time schooling, appear at meal times and then shoot off across the fields. The school has approached SPE for funds to erect a high fence round the school to keep pupils in. The request is refused.

In Jinja the number of street children has grown since my last visit. According to organisations working with them, some children do truant from school to beg from tourists and return home at night, but others have run away and have little choice but to live rough. They hang around in small groups, begging and running off when threatened by irritated shopkeepers. There are efforts to reconnect street children with their families, or if that is not possible, to give them shelter and an education, but the numbers still grow. While I was away a young street child jumped to touch the illuminated sign outside a restaurant, was electrocuted and died.

Rumour has it that before the Queen arrived for the Commonwealth Heads of Government Meeting in Kampala, beggars and vagrants were scooped off the streets and transported to places where they wouldn't be an embarrassment. There is no proof of this but what Arnold Schwarzenegger did in California, Africa may well do too. SPE is looking at working on projects with a Dutch organisation running a drop-in centre, food and counselling for the children, most of whom are very disturbed. A games event is being organised by several organisations and as many volunteers as possible are being rounded up to provide some fun in a safe environment.

I catch sight of Mama Joyce. Prossy is still in hospital in Kampala because she has developed serious weakness in her arms and legs and cannot use them properly. Mama has been to see her for three days and hopes she will be home in around a fortnight. Claire the beautiful lively waitress, who made my first stay so enjoyable is no longer to be seen. When I ask after her in the restaurant I am told that she has returned to the family village in the Sudan. That is all anyone knows.

Technology is moving on apace. Last time I was here the computer room at Amagezi had four old computers which were always free unless there was a school class in progress.

Now thanks to the Mormon Church we have four new Dell computers and no, we don't have to teach creationism as part of the deal. A community class has been running for around six months and people who have passed a basic proficiency test can now come up and practise on a computer out of school hours.

Along with the computers we have been promised a puppet theatre and puppets, which will be put to good use. One Saturday afternoon I was thinking about doing some washing when I had a phone call saying that representatives of the Mormon Church were on their way with the puppet theatre and needed to be greeted accordingly. Nobody was available and as I was already more or less on site would I nip up to Amagezi for a spot of meeting and greeting?

Sitting on the wall is Cibbi who also had the misfortune to answer his phone. We sit around kicking our heels for half an hour with Cibbi threatening to go home. Eventually a four by four drives round the corner and out steps a middle-aged couple who, according to their name tags are Father Bean and Sister Bean. Both are immaculately dressed. Father Bean is sporting a crisp white shirt and tie, while Sister Bean is wearing a sharply pleated mid-calf skirt with her grey hair styled in a neat helmet. As Cibbi unloads the goods my mind turns to the radio programme *I'm Sorry I Haven't a Clue* and late arrivals at the vegetable ball.

Here is the eminent surgeon Sir Kidney Bean with his alcoholic wife Baked Bean, their naïve daughter Green Bean, their au pair French Bean, a cousin from South America Chilli Bean and their uncle a keen disciplinarian called Flageolet Bean. The game goes round in my head, long after our visitors have left. I think I need to get out more.

Local wildlife is proving interesting. Frogs are taking over my banda. Whether it is the same one or dozens of them popping in for a splash in my shower and a snooze under my bed, I am not sure. All I know is that it's not worth capturing them in the washing up bowl and putting them outside because they make it back home under the dilapidated door before I do.

Yesterday walking through the village I saw an amazing sight—seven or eight baby chickens, all a bright shocking pink. When I plucked up courage to mention what I had seen, I found out psychedelic babies are quite common. Birds of prey swoop down and pick off tiny creatures and in the opinion of the locals, bright colours put them off, so they dip baby chickens in a dye bath to help preserve their stock.

I seem to be seeing a fair bit of the Ugandan medical system recently and vow never to moan about the NHS again. Having become friendly with Stella and Tarvine, we have talked about possible investigation into the cause of his deafness.

Trying to find out more about Tarvine's hearing problem, the three of us set out at crack of dawn to make the journey to Kampala. It is a Friday and when we arrive at Mulago Hospital, outpatients is closed and we are given a number and told to come back the following Monday.

When we finally make it into the children's assessment ward we find it heaving with sick children, their parents, brothers and sisters, grandparents and aunts. Every half hour or so a nurse comes out and shouts a few numbers. This is worrying as they barely reach double figures and we are one hundred and twenty seven. A long queue forms outside the laboratory equipment store, which is a walk-in cupboard. I assume they are queuing for tests then realise somebody has a primus stove in there and is cooking chapattis. Heaven knows what is going on in the dirty linen room.

Eventually Stella tells a nurse our number seems to be incorrect and we are given another—87. All we need is a referral to the ear nose and throat unit, but we have to wait our turn. When we are finally called, Stella explains Tarvine is deaf, the doctor claps his hands behind his back, agrees and gives us the referral note.

We are escorted to the unit by a friendly patient who keeps stopping people to tell them I am a muzungu. We are met by a nurse who informs us that the hearing test staff have left and we must come back tomorrow. We explain that we have taken the dawn journey from Jinja twice already and I begin to feel ground down by the misery of it all.

The nurse returns to say Tarvine can be seen and ushers us into an interview room where the radio is blasting out *What a friend we have in Jesus*. It all seems so ironic: sick children, penniless people, hours of queuing in a hospital which was once a showpiece in Africa and is now well past its best, Stella exhausted, Tarvine terrified. To my embarrassment I feel tears welling up and running down my cheeks.

Tests show that Tarvine would benefit from hearing aids and we are given the address of a private clinic. Off we go across Kampala where we find the audiologist who recommended the hearing aids is the very person who is selling them. I begin to have my doubts about the expedition, but Tarvine and Stella had had their hopes raised and I have to see it through.

Volunteers

$\mathcal{S}$OON IT IS my turn to sample Ugandan medical care. I arrange to meet a group of volunteers at Nile River Explorers, the local bar and hub of Bujagali nightlife. It is a place I try to avoid as the atmosphere can turn on a sixpence. The place is frequented by testosterone charged kayakers both local and muzungu. Fights break out with monotonous regularity and sodden muzungus find it highly entertaining to climb on a table and strip off. Much as I dislike the place there's a birthday to celebrate and I arrive later than the rest for a celebratory drink.

Rushing over to greet the group I slip on the sand, which has been sprinkled on the floor and end up lying under a table. Thank God for Cibbi who rushes over and takes me to a corner of the garden away from the drinkers. Someone hands me a brandy, which I drink and am immediately sick. Cibbi finds a mate with a car and together they lift me in, drive the five hundred yards to my banda and deposit me on my bed. All the time Cibbi keeps up a lively chat with his friend assuring him how well he knows me and making it clear I should be treated with respect.

The following day I can't put any weight on my foot and so I summon a boda to the Soft Power Health clinic on the other side of the village. There I am told I need an X-ray and to go to a Medical Centre in Jinja, where an obliging man takes down my details, ushers me into a shed and X-rays my leg. He then shakes his head and tells me it's a mess. I point out it has been a mess for eight years, ever since I broke it in

Greece, but he insists I need to see an orthopaedic doctor. Half an hour later a large, well dressed man bustles in and tells me he is very well qualified and has left his patients at another hospital to rush over and see me. He has looked at my X-rays and has made his diagnosis. I need a half leg plaster, a tetanus injection, antibiotics and pain killers.

I suggest that as nothing appears to be freshly broken, a crepe bandage might do the job. Sternly he makes it clear that his professional reputation depends on giving me the full works. This will cost me around forty pounds and I must pay in advance. I have half that amount with me. He mulls this over and comes up with a solution. He will put the plaster on and lend me a pair of crutches. He will hold back on the tetanus, the pain killers and antibiotics until I have been to the bank. To facilitate this arrangement he will personally find me a boda. I am helped to sit side saddle on the boda, plastered leg hanging almost to the ground and off we go to the bank. Once there I crawl up the steps to the cash machine, supported by the boda driver.

Back at the clinic I hand over the money, only for my doctor to tell me I need to go to another health centre for the injections. Unable to face another boda ride I settle for the taxi option. As we pull up I am greeted by the very doctor who treated me earlier, who must have climbed over the back fence to arrive before us.

Remembering the guide book warnings I ask for a new, sealed disposable needle and full of solicitude, the doctor summons a nurse to bring sealed rubber gloves and injection kit to the taxi as I am in far too much pain to move an inch.

When I finally make it home, waiting for me are a pair of excellent crutches tailor-made by the guys at the SPE workshop. Two days later, hobbling along on my crutches I return to Kampala with Stella and Tarvine to collect his hearing aids and we have lunch in Uganda's answer to McDonalds. My entry causes great interest and when the waitress brings our food she asks:

'What is wrong with your foot? Everyone here wants to know.' A healthier response I feel than the averted eyes of home.

In less than a week my plaster is giving me problems. It is extremely tight and the skin under it feels sore and sensitive. I visit a friendly pharmacist in Jinja with his interesting array of stock including skin lighteners and virginity cream and ask for the plaster to be cut off. He insists on ringing a doctor for advice and putting the phone down tells me his contact is a leading orthopaedic doctor. I steel myself in readiness for a familiar face to appear asking for more money. Luckily my specialist doctor has other patients to tend and for a fiver I am free of his handiwork.

On my way home I am stopped by an elderly man, bent almost double with a twisted leg. He smiles and asks in traditional fashion after my health. He comments on my lack of plaster and I tell him my leg is healed. He seems genuinely delighted. I ask after him. He is not too well he says. His leg is always painful and now the pain has spread up his back. He was run over many years ago and could never afford medical treatment. It is a problem but he thanks God because it could be worse. Smiling he tells me once again how delighted he is to see me so much better. 'God is good' he says.

In the last ten years over two thousand volunteers have spent anything from a day to several months working for SPE. Many like me find themselves drawn back again and again.

Volunteers find SPE through word of mouth, the internet or purely by chance and they are the life blood of the organisation. Like many it was chance that found me in Uganda. Ovarian cancer is called the silent killer because often there are no symptoms until the condition is well advanced. One week I was on the Greek island of Ikaria enjoying a fortnight's holiday with my husband, happy and relaxed. Three weeks later I was having a radical hysterectomy and a few days after that I was being told that my cancer was advanced and I could expect to live around three years with chemotherapy and around six months without it.

My schedule should have been busy with business deadlines to meet. I handed these to a friend and coped a day at a time. With wonderful irony the week my cancer was diagnosed I inherited some money from an uncle. For the first time I had some spare cash, but no time to spend it. We bought a house in France on the top of a hill with breath taking views across the valley, a place where I felt I could live in peace for whatever time was left.

Then came a second thunderous blow. My husband had made some friends on a cycling holiday and they were all coming out to stay. There were five or six, well two or three. In fact there was one who came by special invitation, ticket booked online by my husband. Their behaviour left me in no doubt what was going on.

She left and I begged and cried for hours. Finally he said he had to be alone and caught the next flight to Ireland and to her. I returned to England where I took to drinking gin, and counting sleeping pills. I needed to get away but where? A holiday alone was the last thing I needed. The idea of voluntary work came to mind and I started to look online. There was plenty of choice: teaching in Thailand, building in Ceylon. My children were unsure and warned me of the money being made from bleeding hearts like mine. I asked a friend who had been involved with VSO if she could help and she made enquiries, coming up with three suggestions: a street theatre group in Romania, a children's village in Tanzania and SPE.

The theatre group turned out to be evangelical which was not for me. The children's village did not reply and Hannah from SPE sent a quick reply saying 'You're welcome, come when you like, stay as long as you like'. When I pointed out my shortcomings, the reply was brief. 'Why don't you get on a bloody plane and come?'

All volunteers over twenty five have a story, which drives us to seek out new adventures and make new relationships with people we would never meet at home. We work for nothing, pay our own airfares, accommodation and food. Just about everyone who has done it would say it is worth every penny.

We come in all ages, shapes and sizes. Some know exactly what to expect while others take a while to acclimatise. Jan who became a good friend, took her luggage into her banda and enquired where she could plug in her heated rollers. Within a day and a half she was working hard in one of the pre-schools, running art and craft sessions and demonstrating to Ugandan staff the concept of learning through play. Elegant and amusing, she left behind her husband, children and grandchildren to bring some colour and creativity into classrooms, where lessons rely heavily on chalk and talk even when the pupils are barely four years old.

Jenny from the Australian Gold Coast, first came out to Africa several years ago with her nephew Ryan and spent a day painting with SPE. She went home, took an English for Speakers of Other Languages course and saved, working in a day job in finance and in the evenings in her brother-in-law's seafood restaurant. For several years she has spent six months in Uganda and six months saving for the next trip. Staff and diners in the restaurant collect money in a box, which pays for the secondary education of several local children. Over the years Jenny has made close friends among the villagers, who love her enthusiasm and dedication.

Her classes are for women only, as many would be too embarrassed to attend mixed classes. Many of her pupils have never been to school, yet with Jenny's support they quickly learn and are keen to try out their English. Their confidence grows with their skills and Jenny has to work hard to keep up with demand. Some want to learn English to improve their job chances, others to help their school age children.

One pupil explained, 'My husband would not allow me to attend our son's graduation. He said I would be an embarrassment because I didn't speak English'.

When I was asked to keep an eye on volunteers working in the village, to welcome them and see that they settled in and enjoyed their stay, it didn't seem like an onerous task! First of all I had underestimated Shaz the SPE manager's ability to sound enthusiastic when repeating the same facts for the fiftieth time. Also I had no idea of the undercurrents that wash around the world of volunteering.

Most volunteers quickly become part of the team, but some do not. There was the middle aged man from Ontario who had signed on for three days. He survived my introductory talk, jumped in a taxi and headed back to Kampala.

Within days I hit my first cultural problem. Several of the girls complained that one of the Ugandan interns, (young people on a short-term paid work experience contract), had been making embarrassing sexual comments.

Internships are like gold dust to locals as they can lead to a valuable reference or even a permanent job.

I meet Cibbi to talk over the matter and he points out that even after years of working with muzungus he still often feels unable to gauge situations. He hears jokes and conversations among volunteers, relaxing in the evening, which would be considered offensive to Ugandans, but which result only in a good laugh. His view is that the intern, faced with what he sees as sophisticated, worldly wise muzungu girls in their strappy tops and brief shorts, has misread the situation completely. Cibbi says he will have a word with him and it works. No more complaints there, thank goodness.

However a couple of days later I am shocked when I hear from Eithne that some volunteers feel I am not distributing the work fairly. Apparently volunteers who have just arrived see the best jobs, such as helping Jan at the pre-school, are already taken. This takes me by surprise as the preschool work came up before the second batch of volunteers arrived. However I begin to see volunteers need to be consulted frequently and given as much freedom as possible to decide how to spend their time. After all many have saved for months for the trip and foregone several holidays in the process.

There are occasions when with the best will in the world one cannot bridge the gap between expectation and reality. Long-term volunteers usually have advance email contact with Shaz outlining their interests and experiences and drawing up a draught project for when they arrive, but sometimes despite strenuous efforts, the match is not quite right.

Jane and Don were friends travelling out together. Jane was experienced in child protection and had agreed to work with a member of staff at the education centre to draw up a much needed child protection policy, while Don, with his enthusiasm for carpentry, was to run a month long project teaching young people basic woodwork skills.

News of the latter had been greeted with enthusiasm by local young people. They had applied in writing, followed by an interview. Twelve of them had appeared in their best clothes, dripping with perspiration and shaking with nerves. To them the course represented an opportunity to learn the basics of a trade.

On arrival Jane and Don seem surprised to find their email correspondence has been taken so seriously. Jane isn't sure she wants to be involved in protection issues. She wants to teach. This is difficult. SPE does not place volunteers in teaching posts in primary or secondary schools. This is because muzungu accents are not understood by local children; also volunteers taking over a class for a few weeks means lack of continuity and long term volunteering might mean a Ugandan teacher losing a job.

I explain this and stress the need for help with the child protection policy. Jane is not impressed. She wants to teach. Eventually I say I will ring the deputy head of a local primary school to see if he can help, but that I am not doing this under the SPE umbrella and she will be working strictly on her own.

I have doubts about this move but we seem to have reached an impasse and time is moving on. It all turns out for the best. Jane loves the school and they love her. She sorts out their pupils, sets up a charity to support the school and has a friend design them a website. Meeting her later she tells me all she has done and offers to write an article for the SPE website encouraging other people to come out and teach!

Don is shocked to find there is a group of young people awaiting him. Carpentry is only a hobby. He hasn't got many tools. He wouldn't know where to start. A month is a long time and he might like to try different projects rather than just one. We talk matters over and he agrees to meet the group, look at the materials and start working on making benches for the education centre. I phone Shaz with my concerns and she says Don needs to realise he can't let the young people down. The first session goes well. Don knows much more than he gives himself credit for and begins to relax. I am enthusiastic but still he is unsure and this pattern continues for three weeks, with Don threatening to leave and me talking him round.

Then in the middle of the third week he breaks the news that he is off on safari, so will be unable to complete the course. Shaz suggests I find a local carpenter and SPE will pay him to complete the last week.

I ask around and am given the name of a man who does work at a kayaking operation in town. I find the place and ask to speak to Mohammed the carpenter. The infuriated muzungu behind the desk shrieks at me that he is employed there fulltime. She is fed up with him disappearing to do work for other people and will I please clear off.

After what seems a futile search I hear about Abdullah and find his mobile phone number. We agree to meet in Jinja and I feel I am on to a winner. He knows the centre, has a good idea of what is needed and agrees to come up to talk to Don and meet the trainees.

At Amagezi I introduce Abdullah to everyone and am impressed with the way he settles in. That evening I chat matters over with Eithne and say how I feel Abdullah is a good choice: sensible, mature, good at his job, unlikely to cause any problems.

Eithne passes me her mobile phone. She has a text message.

'You have wonderful blue eyes. I am in love with you. Run away and marry me please? Abdullah.'

Pre-schools

*E*ITHNE CANNOT RESIST sharing the message with Florence, who is something of an expert on Ugandan men. In her thirties Flo is lively, beautiful, and a good business woman who is regarded with disapproval by some of the women in the village. She walks with a proud sway of the hips and loves experimenting with her hair. Recently she had it dyed ginger, in a shade so bright that when I saw a shock of red hair bobbing behind a boda driver, I shouted 'Hi Fergus' thinking it was an Irish colleague, only to discover it was Flo. Unlike many Ugandan women who consider trousers to be immodest, she loves them and has a particularly lively tartan pair with gold thread running through them.

Life is not easy for Flo and she works hard. Her three children are all away at school and to fund their education she takes in muzungu lodgers and does their washing. She cleans at the campsite, runs a stall selling goods made by the women's co-operative and offers excellent massages, a skill she learned on the short course run by a volunteer. It is Flo who, when she hears I have a new granddaughter, weaves her an anklet to bring her good fortune.

Flo loves parties and throws one for Steve a long term volunteer when it's his birthday. She insists on slaughtering her one and only turkey and to thank her for her generosity we club together and buy her a bottle of Jack Daniels. Not a direct replacement for the turkey but it helps its memorial service go with a swing.

Her advice to Eithne, after she has rolled about with infectious laughter, is not to pin her hopes on Abdullah for the romance of a lifetime as he almost certainly has several wives already. She offers to find out his details, but Eithne tells her not to bother.

A short time later Jan and I decide to spend a day sightseeing in Kampala. First we head off to the burial place of the kings, a UNESCO World Heritage Site. It comprises a huge thatched hut where some of the Kabakas or Ugandan kings are buried. A slow trickle of people come in, prostrate themselves in front of the curtain which marks the burial spot and walk out backwards. At the side of the room a couple of elderly women are having a sleep on the floor. I assume they are locals who have dropped in with their shopping to take the weight off their feet, but we are told they are from the same tribe as the present Kabaka's chief wife and as such are privileged to come and guard the tomb.

The guide gives us a talk during which we are required to sit with our legs to one side in order not to offend the Kabakas' remains. The present Kabaka has a chief wife and four lesser wives, which is a distinct improvement on his great grandfather who had eighty six wives but only a hundred and twenty four children. He and his chief wife were always carried shoulder high by servants. If the bearers slipped and dropped the royal couple they were slaughtered, so not a job for the faint hearted. Luckily the missionaries came along and stopped such heathen habits. After that the Kabakas saw the light and sent their sons to Eton, Cambridge and Sandhurst.

When Uganda gained independence in the 1960s the then Kabaka was made president, but was soon deposed by Milton Obote, who was ousted in turn by Idi Amin. Obote managed a brief comeback after Amin went into exile, before being finally defeated by the present president Yoweri Museveni. Today the tribal kings of Uganda have no real power, but still have a great following among their subjects.

Shaking our stiff limbs we walk backwards gingerly but reverently down the aisle and out of the burial place, only for Jan to cause an upset by taking her vile female body into the drum store, which only males can enter. With a certain amount of relief we retire to Woolworths, Kampala's only department store, where they have no problem at all with females.

The next Sunday Jan and I accept a long standing invitation to attend a service at a Pentecostal church in the village. As we walk in a member of the congregation asks if we are born again to which we are forced to say no. For the first half hour the minister seems to be suffering from an extended epileptic fit, throwing himself around, shrieking and stabbing himself with his fingers. According to Harriet the Ugandan girl next to us, he is re-enacting Christ emerging from the tomb.

Finally exhausted, the minister sinks into a seat and we have 'praising' with everybody dancing and swaying to drums, repeating phrases such as 'Jesus you are number one.' The drum beat and the voices have a much greater effect than I am expecting and I feel quite emotional for the rest of the day. It takes a boat trip down the Nile to see the birdlife, to recover.

For most rural Ugandans it is impossible to imagine being anything but a believer, with buwidgee tucked away as an insurance when the situation becomes dire. It is quite usual to be asked about one's faith and such questions are not considered in any way intrusive. Although around ten per cent of Ugandans are Moslem, it is assumed that muzungus are Christian. Locals ask me frequently if I am Catholic,

Protestant or 'born againee'. Missionaries, mostly American, abound, usually preaching from impressive churches built with donations from home and often situated next to huts where children are dying for want of a mosquito net.

Homosexuality is illegal and is regularly denounced from the pulpit as a sin. There are calculated to be around half a million gay people in a population of thirty one million, but homophobia is rife. Encouraged by a handful of right wing US evangelists, the message is sent out that gays are paedophiles. Amnesty International has reported the torture and abuse of suspects and there are regular attempts to pass legislation making homosexual acts a capital offence, with imprisonment of up to fourteen years for anyone failing to report gay Ugandans to the authorities. The Ugandan government faces a dilemma. If it passes such draconian laws it risks losing international aid. If it fails to do so it will lose support at home.

God is never far away. When I walk with Tarvine past the Catholic church he stretches out his arms, and pulls an agonised face re-enacting the crucifixion, before running off laughing. Sundays used to be my day of rest, a time to wash out my unmentionables and dry them discreetly on a hedge when nobody was about. Then it was time to sit outside my banda with my book and my knitting. That was until I attracted the attention of the gardener.

'How are you?'

'I am fine how are you?'

'I am well. I have been to church.'

"That's nice.'

'Have you been to church?'

'No, not this morning?'

'Why not?'

'Um I think I got up late and had things to do.'

'God grieves when you don't go to church.'

'Oh dear, yes, well . . .'

'You could go now. Be quick. Straight away.'

Defeated I disappear inside.

God is not just for Sunday. The owner of the campsite has a notice on the back window of his car:

'This car is covered by the blood of the Lord Jesus'. It probably beats central locking in this part of the world.

SPE's two pre-schools have been running for five years taking the poorest children in the villages of Kyabirwa and Buwenda. In order to assess the value of the pre-schools and look at ways in which they might be improved, a group of volunteers, including me, are to carry out a survey tracing the progress of former pupils.

A major problem is that no written records are kept by the pre-schools and very few by the primary schools. Finding a child depends on a teacher having personal information about a pupil and given the large number of children in a class, they often know very little about their pupils' background.

We start by interviewing the head teachers; Justine Nabwami and Florence Mukunya, who make lists of former pupils and where possible the names of the schools they believe they are attending. Contact is then made with eleven local primary schools to try to trace the progress of the pupils. At the same time a list of children believed not to be attending school is drawn up to find out what has happened to them.

What follows is several weeks of detective work by volunteers, checking names against class lists, checking exam results and positions in class, then setting up interviews with teachers to garner opinions on individual progress and former pre-school pupils in general. The overall opinion is that children are well prepared for primary school when they arrive and where family circumstances allow regular school attendance they progress well. The overwhelming request from primary school teachers is that pre-schools should develop pupils' reading and writing skills. The concept of learning through play is unheard of in Uganda. A mark of the good reputation of the pre-schools is the number of teachers asking that their own children be guaranteed places.

Sixteen families with children who attended the pre-schools but are not currently in primary school, are interviewed. The findings reveal in harsh relief the hardships faced by many families.

The first grandmother has no husband. Her daughter is in Kampala looking for work while she looks after her two children both of whom attend school. Her son is 'mentally unwell' and so she is also bringing up his two children. Neither of the son's children is at school because there is no money for uniform or fees.

There are two children in the next family plus three adults: grandmother, sister-in-law and sister. They are all supported by the grandmother who owns a small plot of land. The older child, a girl attends school but the younger child has had to leave.

Other grandparents are raising five orphaned children. One child, a boy attends primary school, but there is no money to educate the others.

Two school age children in another family were in school until six months ago when the father was badly burnt. He has been in hospital ever since and the mother is raising the family alone. Two families have fathers sick with HIV Aids and unable to work.

The burden on grandparents is huge. In another family the grandmother is bringing up two granddaughters because their father is dead and their mother has left. The older child did attend school for a short time but has been sick for the past month and money has run out.

Fifteen children are being brought up by one set of grandparents, because their various parents have died from HIV Aids. The family grows crops and has some chickens. At one time two children did attend primary school but now the grandparents have so many mouths to feed that education is out of the question.

Only one family of the sixteen interviewed has both parents fit and supporting the family. Families try to survive in circumstances almost beyond belief. With practically no money they struggle wherever possible to send at least some children to school. The choice of who receives an education does not seem to depend upon gender. Usually it is the older children who are already attending school who are kept on as long as money will allow.

All the families feel that pre-school provided an excellent beginning to the children's education and raised awareness of the importance of attending school, even when this proved to be an impossibility. Even those in the direst circumstances expressed the hope that at some point they would be able to send their children back to school. It is clear that most families live so near the edge that any misfortune: death, illness, desertion or the arrival of more dependent family members, pushes them into near destitution.

Special Needs

$\mathcal{T}$HE UGANDAN GOVERNMENT has attempted to ban bodas from the centre of Kampala because around eighty per cent of injuries at Mulago hospital are caused by boda accidents. Apparently nobody has taken any notice of the ban and the motorbikes continue to dodge around the cars halted by the Kampala gridlock. In Jinja one or two drivers are renting new gleaming bikes, but the majority lean on the old familiar rust buckets waiting for trade. I have set myself the minimum standard of rear mirrors with glass in, before I clamber on.

There are still a worrying number of ragged children on the streets and recently a member of staff leaving a coffee bar after his evening shift, found a woman giving birth to triplets in the neighbouring alley. In Bujagali Mama Joyce's granddaughter Prossy is making progress, but her illness has affected her sight and she is blind. After months in hospital she has a place at Spire Road, a school for blind children in Jinja. There is still no news of Claire who seems to have disappeared completely.

I am invited to lunch with Stella and Tarvine's family. Tarvine is struggling with his hearing aids. He occasionally seems to hear loud noises such as car engines but very little else.

Stella and Tarvine are back in the family home where there is a fair sized plot of land and little need to buy anything except cooking oil. Living at home are Mary who is academically very bright, taking a lab technicians' course and keen to take my blood to test it for malaria; Lydia and Teddy, twins aged fourteen in the first year of secondary school and Stella who blotted her copybook by becoming pregnant. Stella is doing a catering course run at the government college where students are promised a job when they finish. This seems questionable as so many young people are completing the course, but it is certainly a step forward for her. Originally she had hoped to train as a nurse. After Tarvine was born she returned to school to take her exams, but her leaving grades were not good enough for nursing.

Stella's father is adamant that she should do the catering course and Stella is so relieved to be taken back home she would agree to anything. Her father speaks quite good English and tells me that he has educated his daughters because in Uganda women are helpless unless they have an education whereas men are physically strong and can find labouring work. Elizabeth the mother speaks little English but has started the classes run by Jenny. Much of the time she spends in the smaller outside hut where the cooking is done over an open fire, helped by her daughters and granddaughter Nowella who is staying with the family because her mother is 'finding life hard'. Drinking water is drawn once or twice a day from a standpipe about five minutes walk away. Washing of bodies and clothes is done in the river.

Before eating I am offered bottled water, Coca Cola, Fanta or Stoney's Tanga Wizzy, the latter being Stone's Ginger Beer which is enjoying a new lease of life in Africa. I ask for Fanta and after around twenty minutes Lydia arrives out of breath and clutching a bottle. I realise too late that family resources run to only one muzungu drink and Lydia has run to the trading centre to buy it. The meal is so huge

I manage about half of it, conscious that it almost certainly constitutes the family's rations for a week. Eating is a lonely process as I am given a stool, an honour usually awarded to males while females sit on the floor and I am left alone in the hut while everyone else gathers outside.

Once I have finished, the girls and their mother return and the air begins to sparkle. They are full of funny stories told in good humour against each other. The fact that Lydia who is tiny and slender wants to join the police, is regaled with great hilarity. They all have beautiful voices and sing songs in several parts each holding the notes perfectly.

I have read an article in one of Uganda's two serious newspapers, either *New Vision* or *The Monitor* entitled 'Are you building a house for his second wife?' The journalist points out that if a young couple both with jobs, marry and spend their earnings on building and furnishing a home, should the marriage fail, the house becomes the property of the husband. Advice is for the wife to keep copies of all bills she pays during the marriage but even so there is a warning that the settlement is likely to be in the man's favour.

The girls have strong opinions on women's rights. They assure me that life is different for educated women in Kampala and that they certainly intend to have a more equal relationship with their husbands than their mother has with their father. However they admit that if they married and their husbands took second wives they would have to accept the situation. With a cynicism springing from her own experience Stella announces firmly 'Men wander as soon as the children start to arrive'.

The subject turns to stepmothers of whom there are many and who generally have a bad press. There are kind stepmothers and I know at least two in the village who are bringing up stepchildren as if they are their own. But in a country where hardship is commonplace such generosity is not widespread. Mary is adamant that 'A child's hope of happiness dies with the death of the mother.'

After the weekend I head for the Amagezi Education Centre The centre now has an all Ugandan staff and Venus has recently taken over as general manager.

I am working as a 'gopher' for Sarah. She has come out from the UK where she was deputy head teacher of a school for children with special educational needs, in order to set up provision for children in the Budondo subcounty of Jinja. Her energy and enthusiasm are infectious and her first task is to look at existing provision in the area and to make contact with training organisations.

Having a child with any form of disability here is a financial burden and a social disgrace. Poor families need children to work from an early age, either in the fields or at home looking after younger brothers and sisters. An unproductive ailing family member puts extra pressure on limited resources. Also it is a widely held belief that such children are meted out to parents, usually mothers, as punishment for their sins.

Sarah has already learned of Anna a young girl of around five years with multiple handicaps. Her mother works for SPE and every day has no choice but to shut Anna and her six year old sister in their hut for around four hours. The family needs the money to keep alive and there is nobody except the sister to look after Anna. Sarah has been to see the family and has put up pictures and mobiles to provide some stimulation. She has also arranged for Anna to have physiotherapy from a volunteer to try to give her some movement in her very deformed limbs.

The first day we visit a school with a deaf unit. Finding out information is not easy. Ugandans are not accustomed to UK accents, so find us difficult to understand. They are by nature polite and dislike confrontation, so try hard to tell us what they feel we would like to hear.

'How many deaf children live in the school?'

'There are eight.'

'How many boys and how many girls?'

'Four boys and four girls.'

'So there are two dormitories with four children in each.'

'No one has five children.'

'So are there five deaf boys or five deaf girls?'

'No only four.'

'Who is the extra child in the dormitory?'

'He is a boy.'

'Why is he there?'

'He is lame, but perhaps his father will take him to the hospital when he is older.'

In the deaf unit there are around twenty five children aged from five to eighteen all in one group being taught by Victoria, an assistant who is herself deaf. She signs to Sarah that the teacher is ill. She also signs that the money paid by parents of deaf children for their education is being misappropriated. This we soon realise is a common problem with funding for special needs education. Money from parents, governments, charities or NGOs is often diverted to other areas, which are regarded as more productive and deserving. The children are then put into classes of over a hundred with no extra help, under the name of integration.

Victoria is trying hard, but it is impossible to keep the attention of such a wide age group.

She writes numbers on the board in groups of five, some upside down, some back to front with only one number written correctly. The children then have to copy the numbers and circle the one that is correct. Around five children are following the lesson while the older ones do nothing and the younger ones push each other off their seats. Sarah starts signing to the group and discovers several have good signing skills. Meanwhile I try to stop the youngest stealing my sunglasses.

Our next stop is to see Lydia the inspector of special needs education in the Jinja area. She is polite but determined. Sarah shows her a computerised form she has designed to record details of children. Lydia has a hand written one and prefers hers. No matter how many times Sarah explains that her form would save us a lot of work, Lydia politely changes the subject to indicate that the matter is closed. It is finally agreed that we should attend a meeting of teachers who have filled in Lydia's form and ask them to fill ours in on the spot.

We visit the centre for training special needs teachers at Uganda National Institute of Special Education, part of the University of Kyumbogo on the edge of Kampala. The campus is large and impressive. The course covers visual and hearing impairment as well as learning difficulties which is called mental retardation. There is a growing awareness and interest in autism, but no training available at the moment.

We are invited to sit in on a lecture given by a senior tutor and attended by around one hundred students. They are being questioned on their homework. They have been given twelve acronyms and told to find out what they stand for and the role of each organisation. It scarcely seems to be degree level research. The lecturer focuses her attention on around six keenies at the front whose hands are constantly waving in the air, while the rest look bored or worried that they might be asked something they don't know. At one point the lecturer asks a student to write the answers on the board while she phones a mate. In an hour they get through four acronyms and are told the lecture will continue the following day.

That night we stay at the Sunburst Holiday Home. It is immaculately clean and completely empty except for Sarah and me and the girl running it. There is a pleasant dining room with matching cutlery and tablecloths, which is strange because no meals are provided. Half way through the evening our landlady becomes bored with our company and goes home after locking us in.

Still reeling from yesterday's poor standard of teaching, we head back to the university the next morning. We sit in on an excellent signing class run by a brilliant guy who puts so much energy into his signing it is as good as a theatrical performance. He gives the group a short cartoon strip telling a story, signs it to them, then divides them into pairs with instructions to sign the story to each other. I can now sign 'poor' and 'thinking' and 'beginning' and 'woman'.

In the afternoon we visit a special needs unit attached to the university. All the teachers are at a meeting and eight children have been left with two helpers. At one time the unit took visually and hearing impaired children but the parents have taken many of the children away leaving only the children with 'mental retardation'. The assistants sit and chat while the children wander around feeding each other wax crayons.

Back in Jinja, our next visit is to Spire Road School for the Blind, run by a nun, Sister Regina. She is hard working and committed to the children, who are taught Braille by an inspiring teacher who is himself blind. Even here there is a depressing similarity to other special needs schools. The unit has two working braille machines plus a third, which is broken. There are three children about to take public exams who each need a machine.

A nun from Sister Regina's order runs a drop-in centre three times a week for people with special needs. It is held in a half built church a few miles away and we catch a matatu from the central bus station. Finding the right vehicle is a matter of luck. There are no signs and while everyone is helpful, opinions about which vehicle to take differ widely. We are just about the last passengers to clamber into the fourteen seater van weighed down with twenty or so people squashed together with spare tyres and bags. The woman next to me has a tiny baby and a chicken pecking its way out of a basket. Finally satisfied that there is no more room, the driver orders his 'conductor' to tie the door with string and off we go. Everyone is polite and good humoured, making no fuss about climbing out half a dozen times to let passengers on and off. After a few miles the string fastening the door comes loose and a blessed breeze blows through, much appreciated by all except those sitting near the gaping hole. They hang on for grim death to avoid being thrown into the road.

Around forty five people attend the centre with eight or so regulars who never miss a session. One is a gentle dreamy girl in her late teens, who sits humming quietly, rocking her baby and smiling at whoever catches her eye. Her mother is dead and when her father remarried, he and her stepmother pushed her out of the family house to live alone on the edge of the village. Her son was born as the result of a rape and according to the nun the girl is regularly attacked by men and has been given a contraceptive injection to stop her having more children.

The group is making rush mats, learning to sew garments by hand and making rope by plaiting sisal. The aim is to produce work to a standard where it can be sold. As a special treat, which happens around once a month, everyone is given a bottle of soda and a bread roll.

Container City

$\mathcal{P}$RIDE CERTAINLY COMES before a fall. No sooner do I become a seasoned traveller, finding my way round airports, slinging cases nonchalantly on to trolleys and waving my passport in front of officials, than I find myself back in the batty old woman league.

After the obligatory sausage sandwich in De Nile I set off on a boda to the office in Jinja. I jump off, avoiding the searingly hot exhaust like the expert I am and open my rucksack to pay the driver. There is my waterproof folded neatly in readiness for the next downpour. Otherwise my bag is empty: no purse and no glasses.

We retrace our journey in the fond hope that the zip worked its way open and the goods are lying in the road. I go back to my breakfast café—nothing. Thank God my passport is safe, but I have no money and with no cards no means of getting any. I have also lost my brand new reading glasses.

I sit outside the office trying to take in what has happened and to work out a plan of action. First I must phone the bank, cancel my cards and see if they can send me a new one. The answer to that question is a resounding 'no'. It would take weeks and be extremely dodgy. The only solution to my lack of money is for friends to lend me some and for me to transfer the money back to them via phone calls to my bank. Someone suggests putting out a message on the local radio, which results in a single phone call from a guy telling me he has my belongings and will return them if I credit his phone with 10,000 shillings.

Steeling myself I visit the police station to report the loss for an insurance claim and try not to notice the hands waving through the grille of the holding cell. I recount my loss while suggesting strongly the items have been lost not stolen as I don't want the cops' least favourite character to be brought in and roughed up. A policewoman bursting proudly out of her regulation skirt, takes a statement, gives me a form and tells me to have it photocopied twice and bring the copies back so she can fill them in. A power cut in town means I can't return with the forms immediately. Over a coffee I am warned the police will ask for cash and on no account should I pay anything. I'm not too sure I'll hold out under torture or even intense questioning now I've seen the holding cells.

I have no idea how much crime is reported to the police. Security around the SPE office building in town is tight. When I am the last to leave I have to remember to lock up the office, the front door, the back door and the gate. There is an ascari who sleeps in a hut by the front gate, but apparently the last time there was a break in the ascari threw a dustbin lid at the intruders and then ran away. The police heard the crash, thought it was a gun and decided not to investigate too quickly. The intruders made it into the kitchen, didn't seem to fancy the tea bags and packets of dried pasta and cleared off. A few nights ago a German girl renting one of the back rooms awoke to find someone sawing away the iron bars at her window, so now a light has been installed at the back of the building and the ascari instructed to take regular patrols

Much as I enjoy Jinja I relish the fact that after work I can return to the relative peace of Bujagali, where I am greeted by familiar faces and the endearing words, 'well be back'. Although changes are afoot. The long standing rumour about the flooding of the falls as part of a hydro electric power project has become reality and work on the dam which will mean the end of the beautiful Bujagali Falls, is in progress.

I have changed my accommodation and I am staying next door to the campsite with Eithne who is working part-time as a volunteer while managing a quad-biking business for the owners who are in Australia.

Accommodation is centred around the workshop and is cunningly constructed from a variety of containers. One of my walls is the side of a container and there is a small louvred window, which looks straight out on to the workshop sink. I drew my curtains on the first morning and received a cheery wave from a figure inches away scrubbing his overalls.

Container City is quite an achievement. One container is a gift shop. Above the gift shop a bedroom has been built with steps running up the outside. On the other side of the yard are three containers side by side. One is a shed for the bikes, one is a kitchen with a bedroom at the back and a mezzanine level where there is a window, TV, sofa and a few rats that like nothing better than to run in front of the screen. The office is half a container and the loos and shower have a definite container look about them. Sadly they are on the other side of the compound from my room and the place is guarded at night by two dogs and an ascari. I am working on some pelvic floor exercises in the hope that they will strengthen my bladder.

Aware of my lack of fitness I have started swimming with a group of volunteers at a hotel pool in town. Clambering out of the water on to wet tiles I managed to twist my knee. Highly embarrassed I decided to take a taxi home rather than be hauled on to a boda. When the taxi driver arrived he quoted an exorbitant price and although I said I would pay, the others were so incensed they insisted we walk towards town and find a more reasonable driver. We all stalk off, with me struggling to keep up and clinging on to the odd bush for support. Once the driver decided I had provided sufficient entertainment, he caught us up and dropped his price.

Life in the village is not easy for many families. Claire seems to have disappeared. Mama Joyce is in hospital and rumour has it, has had a stroke. She has a large extended family who all rely on her hard work and cooking skills for their survival.

One afternoon I meet Bessie one of Jenny's pupils, who is making such good progress in her English class that we can speak without a translator. She looks tired and worried and confides that her husband has found another woman and after dividing his time between both homes has finally moved out. He is refusing to support them in any way. He has got rid of the chickens that provided much needed cash and is threatening to move his new woman into the house. Bessie is a proud intelligent woman who struggles ceaselessly to keep her family together and humiliation and exhaustion are burned into her face.

Life is not much better down the track. Emmanuel has been a worry to his family for months. Aged fourteen he has lost interest in school and seems to be drifting into bad company. Sensing his lack of commitment his sponsor has withdrawn support in favour of a younger brother. Despite his father's advanced age and difficulty working the family land, Emmanuel is reluctant to help in the fields. Matters come to a head when the parents of a neighbour report him to the police for defilement.

Their daughter and Emmanuel have been caught having sex and the situation is serious. Better suited to abusive relationships where one partner is underage and the other much older, defilement brings with it a heavy prison sentence and Emmanuel finds himself locked in the prison hut in the village awaiting a move to the dreaded holding cell. Then there is a message from the girl's family. They are willing to drop the charges for a sum of money. Angry replies, on the lines that the girl is the village bike and Emmanuel is by no means the only one, do not help. Finally after several days' negotiation, the amount required is lowered and paid by a cousin. Emmanuel returns to the bosom of his very angry family.

Sarah is holding awareness days in local villages to put forward a positive view of people with special needs and to advertise the outreach clinics offering free physiotherapy and occupational therapy sessions. I attend several of these events with a Ugandan teacher called Beatrice. The first trip involves the usual crossed wires and me standing in the wrong taxi park for an hour.

Beatrice has four children and her ambition is to send them all to boarding school where they will be locked up and safe from kidnappers. There has been a great deal in the newspapers about child kidnapping for human sacrifice and black magic rituals and the police are visiting schools talking to children about possible dangers. Staff at the pre-schools have shared concerns about little ones who are taken ill at school but cannot be sent home alone. There is also worry about the beginning and end of the school walk when children are alone.

As in the rest of the world Ugandan newspapers thrive on hair raising stories such as the one featuring a man who allegedly chopped his wife's head off with a panga because she had taken around twenty pence from the table. Villagers were so incensed they tried to lynch him but he was saved by the arrival of the police. Sharing the same page was the account of a high school pupil taking her final exams who was rushed to hospital to give birth, but made it back to school in time to finish the paper.

A recent headline was 'The Season for Female Circumcision is Coming Round Again'. To everything there is a season—a time to plant and yes, well! While female genital mutilation is illegal in Uganda, there are still areas where it is practised despite a government campaign pointing out the lifelong problems it causes. Yet again I turn to my *Bradt Guide*. Here I find mutilation is centred around the Sabiny people in Kapchorwa, Eastern Uganda and until the 1970s girls who refused to undergo the procedure were regarded as outcasts and forbidden to marry. Jane Kuka, the principal of a teacher training college in the area began a campaign to educate women about the dangers of circumcision and won the support of the national government.

Angry that their customs were under attack local leaders passed a bye-law in 1986 requiring all women to be circumcised. Although the law was only in place for a short time, many women were seized and forcibly circumcised. To fight this Jane Kuka set up the Sabiny Elders Association to preserve Sabiny traditions while revealing the health risks associated with circumcision. Thanks to her work the number of women being circumcised has dropped dramatically and is now limited to remote rural areas.

Rumour has it that freedom of the press is being squeezed by a government tired of criticism of its policies. Recently *The Monitor* reported President Museveni has admitted to ghost names on the electoral register and even to ghost polling stations, which is interesting in the run-up to general and presidential elections.

President Museveni's re-election seems pretty well a foregone conclusion. He is still widely respected by Ugandans in the south for bringing relative stability to the country after the Amin years. Yet protests and marches in Kampala are frequent and the last weeks have been particularly noisy, coming to a head when the present Kabaka of Buganda, wanted to attend a rally out of his area and the government refused permission. This caused days of rioting in and around the capital.

A suggestion is that Museveni will offer universal secondary education as a vote winner. It would be a popular move, if the reality were more classrooms and more teachers and a truly free system where pupils did not have to buy a uniform and books and pay into a school fund before entering the premises.

Big news in the press, which is bound to grow bigger is the billions of tons of oil under Lake Albert in the north. There are disputes with the Democratic Republic of Congo, which has laid claim to at least part of the bonanza, but oil could make Uganda or more likely, a few of its citizens, very wealthy indeed.

Back to the present and there is a new face in the office. Sitting opposite me is SPE's new administration assistant. Lilian is a graduate with a business studies degree and has been working as a volunteer at the SEN unit. She is expecting a baby in May but her mother will care for the child while Lilian brings in some much needed money. Her boyfriend has disappeared to the elephants' graveyard where so many reluctant Ugandan fathers take refuge, never to be seen again. Delighted as Lilian is with the job, all is not well. She was an hour early for work on Monday and half an hour late on Tuesday. Shaz her boss was livid and went off to Bujagali without her. It transpires that Lilian's mother lives in Kampala and Lilian having quarrelled with her cousin, has had nowhere to live for the past three nights. With the matron's support but without the head's knowledge she has been sleeping at the special needs unit at a local school. The reason she was late was that the head arrived early and stood in front of the dormitory chatting so Lilian could not make her escape. She now has a room, thank goodness, but it is going to be tough for her.

Once again cultural differences make communication between muzungus and Ugandans awkward. Ugandans find confrontation difficult and will do anything to avoid an angry exchange, often seeming to agree with what is being said, or even saying what they feel is wanted. To a muzungu this can be seen as being devious or dishonest, while to the Ugandan it is simply good manners.

As usual my source of information on all things Ugandan is Cibbi, for whom life has changed dramatically. To everyone's surprise at the age of thirty eight he has found a partner and settled down with Mary, a bright attractive girl from the village and they are expecting a baby. Taking congratulations and ribald comments in his stride, Cibbi smiles and admits his father is greatly relieved. For years he has been telling Cibbi that he is spending far too much time with 'those muzungus and their family planning ways'.

Transport anywhere is not easy at the moment. The mornings tend to be fine, but in the afternoon there is usually a downpour sending red mud sliding down the tracks and making the road into Jinja virtually impassable. We now have dual carriageway on the Bujagali road. It doesn't last the entire three miles in fact it only covers around twenty feet. Where the rains have caused huge ditches in the middle of the road, the locals have put in sugar cane plants. There is also a home grown do-it-yourself road repair service in action. When the rain eases local guys fill in the biggest craters with mud while their mates hold a rope across the road to stop local traffic and collect donations.

Whether mosquitoes come out in larger numbers in the wet weather might be debatable, but at the moment I am covered in bites many of which are splendidly infected and growing by the day to the size of a ten pence piece. Regardless of whether the area is going to be covered by clothes I now spray every square inch in the morning and at sunset. A volunteer who found fresh bites appearing after returning to the UK was told she had an extreme allergic reaction and a lot of the red itchy bumps were not bites but a reaction to the original bites. Personally I cannot believe I could have been bitten so often without noticing it was happening.

Despite the grey clouds I force myself out of bed at 6.30am to go bird watching for a couple of hours. Finding it difficult to tell a thrush from a starling, I had little enthusiasm but joined the party with as good a grace as I could muster and am so glad I did. The guide spoke excellent English and was constantly picking up snatches of song or glances of colour, pointing out something new for us on which to focus our binoculars. In over two hours we barely moved five hundred yards. In that small distance we saw at least a dozen different birds. Plus I learned that the bird that wakes me every morning with a strange song is the African morning dove.

Celebration

*I*T IS TEN years since Hannah Small hit on the idea of offering passengers on her overland truck a chance to spend a day helping to repair a Ugandan primary school while making a donation to cover the cost of materials. Now it is time to celebrate.

The day begins with a festival at the Amagezi Centre. Pupils from schools, which have been renovated and others which use the centre, are there by the dozen with displays of singing and dancing. Guest of honour is the British High Commissioner. His presence recognises the achievements of the past decade, but I have to admit to a touch of disappointment. If one is bearing the white man's burden for Her Britannic Majesty Queen Elizabeth 11 in Sub-Saharan Africa surely one should look the part.

I was expecting spanking whites with gold epaulettes, black knee length boots, a few medals and ostrich plumes plus a bevy of loyal retainers. Instead we have a pleasant young man in shorts and an open necked shirt who looks as if he would be happy to give you a hand if you had a puncture and who in the absence of a retinue of guards has brought his wife and children.

Staff at the art department have made commemoration plates which are duly handed out and Cibbi makes a great speech welcoming everyone and requesting Beda to go home and tell her family in the UK that the King of Scotland is dead and they are all welcome to come back. Beda is a Ugandan Asian paying her first visit to Uganda for thirty seven years and spending six weeks teaching ceramics at the SPE education centre. Born in Jinja, she trained as a teacher, married and taught in a local secondary school. Her relatives, while aware of the anti-Indian feeling around them, were confident they would not be affected because they had a grandmother who was a native Ugandan.

Such confidence proved ill founded and the family was given just a few weeks to settle their affairs and go. According to Beda, because of his affection for Scotland, Idi Amin would only allow Caledonian Airways to carry out the evacuation. This meant hoards of refugees stranded for days at Entebbe Airport. The majority had left virtually everything behind. They had no warm clothes and were doubtful of the reception they would receive in the UK. Beda has returned alone as her husband found the thought of a visit too painful.

In the afternoon a crowd of us blow up scores of balloons for the staff party. Everyone working or volunteering with SPE is invited. The food has been donated by a trustee and we are all given a ticket for a free drink, after that it's buy your own with the profit going to the charity. Whenever muzungus and Ugandans get together for a party there is much hilarity about the way we dance. Ugandans seem to have joints we don't possess and take great delight in pointing out how stiff our bodies are compared with theirs. In the words of one local 'You muzungus like breasts while Africans prefer bottoms'.

Even tiny children seem to be able to move their infant bodies to the beat of a drum and the transformation is mind blowing when a quiet teenage girl, too shy to look an adult in the eye, will tie a shawl around her hips to draw attention to her assets, and dance in an eye wateringly suggestive manner, only to slide back into her seat and stare demurely downwards once the music has stopped.

In the UK it usually takes several bottles of wine, tightly closed curtains and the Beatles, before a group of baby boomers start to bop around. Here people dance as naturally as they walk and no opportunity is missed, even queuing up for needles and yarn means a chance for toe tapping and hip swirling.

There are certainly some amazing bums on display tonight, gyrating like mad to the beat of the drums. While our efforts fail to reach African standards there is nothing like the earth shaking beat of a drum to make the years fall away and loosen stiff muzungu joints.

Hannah makes a speech thanking everyone and recalling the development of SPE from the early days. The emotion is palpable as people exchange glances and hug each other. Every volunteer knows the feeling of hopelessness springing from recognition that the task is too great and the situation too dire for any real progress to be made. The term 'pissing in the wind' is all too meaningful to all of us, but at moments like this there is a swell of optimism and a conviction that with energy and good will, the Soft Power creed of constructive dialogue and peaceful interaction can slowly but surely make a difference. The Quaker maxim of small circles of change comes to my mind.

There is Shaz the general manager, a young languages graduate who has been with SPE for the past five years and accounts for every penny raised as if it were her own. I defy anyone to run a tighter ship than Shaz or to put more enthusiasm into recruiting and organising volunteers.

Once out here they are in the safe hands of Cibbi who keeps them busy painting and decorating by the truckload. In the evening he is off to persuade passing overlanders to give up a day of their holiday, paint like fury, make a donation and buy a t-shirt.

Then there are the two pre-schools, offering playtime plus number and literacy skills for under sixes from the poorest and most disadvantaged families. Every morning small clusters of little ones, barefooted and wearing t-shirts in orange, red or green depending on their class, are to be seen clutching their tiffin boxes and heading for school.

Families are asked to provide food for a mid morning snack to ensure the children have something to eat at least once a day. The other nurseries in the area are all fee paying and way beyond the means of most people, so a few leftovers from last night's evening meal is seen as a good price to pay for free education.

The Amagezi Centre is used almost every day in term time by local school parties and in the holidays for community classes. It is rare to visit the centre and find nothing going on. Local people attend classes there, the shop displays crafts and cards to lure visitors to spend money and the demonstration garden is full of plants growing in dustbins and bags to show how food can be grown in the unlikeliest places.

The women's English as a foreign language classes are being run in two villages by Jenny with women clamouring for the opportunity to prove their skills. The Special Educational Needs project is moving from strength to strength under Sarah who works for less than a tenth of her UK salary. A special needs unit based at a local primary school is up and running with two teachers and dormitory accommodation for twenty children, with fees kept as low as possible by fund raising and government support.

SPE might be tiny but its size means that just about every penny donated hits home where it is needed. We are not about telling people how to live their lives but listening to how they want to move forward. Everyone present echoes Hannah's words 'Here's to the next decade.'

A few days later and I again experience the gap between different cultures.

Four volunteers including me are working with Romeo running disability awareness workshops at a school about four miles north of Jinja. SPE is about to open a special needs class and re-open a class for deaf children and the workshops are to give pupils and teachers an idea of the range of disabilities and to show how people with special needs can learn to live as independently as possible. It may sound basic even condescending to western ears but only last week a Ugandan newspaper ran an article about a school closing because pupils were catching epilepsy from each other.

With the aid of a wheelchair, crutches, and a Braille machine, Romeo makes the point that with help many people with disabilities can live active lives. The first session is with the top class aged anywhere between eleven and eighteen. Volunteers, pupils and teachers are divided into small groups to discuss different issues. The first question my group tackles is the causes of blindness. The first answer from a serious young man is 'Losing your lenses.' The second, more worryingly, is family planning.

On our second day we are greeted by the teachers who ask excitedly if we had noticed a crowd gathered on the main road at the neighbouring village. We had and assumed there had been a traffic accident.

'No' is the reply. 'There was a burning last night.'

'A burning what of?'

'A thief.'

'A thief? You mean a person?'

'Yes he was very bad and had many chances. He had been in prison and never learned his lesson. He was caught stealing corrugated roofing. People were so angry they beat him and then they burned him.'

'You mean he's dead?'

'Of course.'

'Did he die of the beating and then his body was burnt?'

'No he was beaten but he was alive. He was burnt outside his parents' house and he was screaming for his father, but his father would not come out to him because he was too ashamed.'

'Oh my God that's awful to burn someone alive.'

'But he was very bad and would not change his ways and people were very angry.'

'Even so does anyone deserve to be burned alive?'

'He stole from everyone, even when he was a child he was a thief.'

The exchange slithers into an embarrassed silence as it dawns on both sides that a gulf is forming too wide to be crossed. Our hosts are becoming offended that we seem to be judging them to be cruel and uncivilised, while shock at what we have heard is written clearly on our faces.

The group disperses with us all suddenly finding the need to hunt for folders and bags. The matter is not mentioned again until the evening when our small group of muzungus tries and fails to come to terms with the story.

'You have to remember there's no neighbourhood watch out here and no insurance policies to claim on. If somebody steals from you, your children go hungry.'

'Yes but to burn someone alive and to hear their screams is beyond belief.'

'We're not here to sit in judgement on people whose lives are so much harsher than ours. This isn't Tunbridge Wells.'

There is no conclusion to be reached. The burning smoulders in my mind for days as I try to sleep in my banda, aware that a fellow human died in agony only a few miles away.

Knitting

*T*EACHING UGANDAN WOMEN to knit.

The idea grew from a conversation with Sarah as we spent a Sunday afternoon in her flat watching a DVD and I tackled the sleeve of a jumper.

'Why don't you start a knitting group?'

I love knitting and have produced some wild and woolly offerings in my time, but I am no expert. Anyone with a keen eye would see that my stitches are often not even and my workbox is stuffed with strange half finished rejects.

Even if I had the skill to teach some people, what could they knit that would be of use in Sub-Saharan Africa? Where could we sell the finished items? Not least how would I teach women with virtually no English to follow a pattern?

During the following months in the UK I think over the possibility of a knitting group and decide that there is not a great deal to be lost by giving it a go. I ask friends for left over wool and spare needles. The message goes out to village halls, church groups and the Women's Institute. The phone begins to ring and my spare bedroom becomes full of bags. A friend from Northern Ireland and another from Cumbria send large bundles of needles, all thoughtfully sorted into pairs.

Two lovely shops in Bury St Edmunds: *Wibbling Wools* and *Elizabeth Gash* donate yarn and needles and the problem arises of transport. Then somebody comes up with the idea of vacuum storage bags. Used properly they reduce the size of the contents by more than half, but care is needed! Several times I fail to close the seals. I attach the vacuum hose, suck out all the air, admire my handy work only to find five minutes later the bag has regained its original dimensions.

Where to start? My plans are hazy but I have printed off an illustrated A to Z of Knitting from the internet and have collected a folder full of simple patterns for phone cases, hair bands and scarves and if we ever progress far enough—a knitted doll.

I visit Romeo's mother Jane and tell her my plan. Jane is tiny and in her forties. She was married to Peter when she was around fifteen and he was middle aged with a wife and child. Eleven children later, her youngest five years old and the eldest around twenty four, she toils ceaselessly to feed and educate her family. Jane has taken a tailoring course with SPE and has the loan of a sewing machine which has pride of place on her verandah. In the morning she works in the 'shamba' or garden and for the rest of the day, in between scooping up grandchildren and cooking for her family, she sews bags for tourists and clothes for locals. Jane is related to half the village and is on chatting terms with the remainder so she seems like a good place to start with my knitting.

After showing her some samples I explain I am looking for around half a dozen women who would be interested in learning to knit. She tells me to come to her house tomorrow afternoon and she will have spread the word.

The next afternoon a dozen women, aged between about eighteen and fifty, gather in Jane's garden. I cast on some stitches for them one at a time and demonstrate the first knitting stitch with the mantra 'in, round, through, off'. Some are there in seconds, while for others it takes longer, but by our third meeting most people have the right idea, while a number can knit, purl and cast on and off.

Numbers grow daily as word spreads around the village. At this stage it is hard to imagine the group will produce saleable objects, but after a hard morning's physical labour planting and weeding, the chance to wash, change into clean clothes and relax chatting with friends, is inviting.

Newcomers slip in and wait patiently until I notice they are there. As soon as I start to pack my bags at the end of a session, I am besieged by knitters, waving their work for me to sort out their mistakes. Jane's house is at the opposite end of the village to Eden Rock, my current home and it's often a rush to make it back before dark.

Members of the group are keen to follow instructions, but find some of my ideas extremely perplexing. I show them pictures of striped scarves and explain they need to be long so they can be wrapped around the neck to keep out the cold. How long is long? Well long enough to go round the neck three times at least. As knitting grows longer eyes become wider in disbelief that anyone could wear such a cumbersome item.

Knitted slippers arouse much interest. They are not strong enough to be worn outside. When would people wear them? I explain that UK winters are cold and slippers are worn inside the house. The knitters smile politely at a loss to understand how this could happen.

Colours are also an issue. Ugandan women can rarely afford new clothes for their children. Items are handed down or if mothers are relatively wealthy, bought second hand from the market. Even with such limited choice women love to see their children in bright colours which look breath taking against dark skins. Why then would a muzungu mother choose white or pastels, or worse still think navy blue is a good idea when they could have a bright orange and purple baby blanket?

In addition to my village group I teach four SEN pupils at Walukuba School. There are two deaf girls who have caught on quickly and two boys with cerebral palsy. It is hard to devote time to them all as they have such different needs. Eunice a teaching assistant sits in and I try to encourage her to help one of the boys while I move the girls on a step. When I turn round she is knitting away happily and her pupil is fast asleep!

I am invited to spend one day in Kampala with Sarah, Romeo and Diana, an Australian speech therapist, looking at two schools for children with special needs. One was large with purpose-built premises and light airy classrooms taking pupils from all over Uganda and Rwanda. Fees were around eighty pounds sterling a term, which is way beyond what people in our villages could pay. The other school was small and run on a shoestring, offering physiotherapy to children and sewing classes to their mothers. The women have free classes and then the use of a sewing machine for which they pay around twenty pounds a year, so not hugely different from the SPE set-up.

In the afternoon we went into Kampala to try and find Romeo a reasonably priced bike as his had been stolen. Having found one for him, Sarah decided she needed a bike too, so Diana was left holding the first one outside the shop. After fifteen minutes we received a frantic text message from Diana saying she was being hassled with offers of marriage and requests to buy the bike.

After trying other accommodation I really appreciate my return to Eden Rock and my banda. Even though the hot water is a myth and my mosquito net fell down on my head when I was sitting on the bed. The wood used to make the frame had clearly had several different lives before it reached my banda and had quietly collapsed and died. When

I told Fred the manager he nailed some hooks to the wall and stretched the net over them assuring me a carpenter would arrive at crack of dawn the next day.

I am the proud owner of a bar of Imperial Leather soap spotted in a supermarket in Kampala. The insects love it and I regularly pick off corpses which expired experiencing something that was forever England. I also have a very dead cockroach in my loo that refuses to go away. Such incidents fade with Diana's story. She is living with Flo and woke up to find her mosquito net bouncing above her and a rat using it as a trampoline.

Saturday there were big celebrations in Kikaka, a village between Jinja and Bujagali. By mid-morning a crowd had gathered around a group of young men dressed in little other than feather headdresses and flip-flops. The atmosphere was carnival-like, as passers-by were stopped with requests for money. There was to be a tribal adult male circumcision ceremony and the collection was to pay for medical attention should it be necessary. Some of the lads looked worn out after spending several days parading through the neighbourhood. The thought of the coming ordeal must have weighed heavily on them, as behind the shouts and cheers, they look tired and nervous.

Research into my invaluable *Bradt Guide to Uganda* leads me to think the participants are possibly members of the Bagisu clan originally from the Mount Elgon area of Eastern Uganda. Adult male circumcisions take place in alternate years. Young men over sixteen volunteer for the ceremony and travel from village to village to gain support for the event.

The ceremony is public and men are expected to undergo the procedure without moving or making any noise. Afterwards they carry out a ritual dance before being taken off and looked after by friends and family. Men who avoid circumcision are considered cowardly and any unfortunate enough to have wives who denounce their state have been known to be forcibly circumcised, even if they are of an advanced age.

According to my guide book tourists both male and female are welcome at such ceremonies. I decide to give it a miss.

Rarely have I experienced anything other than kindness and good humour in Uganda so I was unprepared for what happened a few days later. I left Steve my boda driver outside Walukuba School where he said he would wait for me. Just over an hour later I came out and he was gone. Realising I would soon be late for my village knitting group, I hailed a flashy looking driver with sunglasses and medallion who assured me he knew where Bujagali was. Five minutes on and he turned to ask if I knew the way. He then stopped on the dual carriageway and called a group of guys over. Nobody knew where Buj was and stupidly I interrupted the debate with an impatient 'For God's sake just take me back to Jinja town'.

Immediately one of the men stepped in front of my nose and shouted 'Do not say the word God in my country. It is blasphemy and you must tell us who is the god you worship.'

Thoroughly shaken I begged the driver to take me into Jinja and we made a hasty exit.

Half a mile up the road and we were overtaken by Steve who had popped into town to buy a pineapple for a friend.

Buliisa

I AM OFF TRAVELLING, leaving the knitters to practise their stitches. Having recently become a trustee of Soft Power Education, I am compiling a trustees' report and as part of this I am going with Shaz to look at the Conservation Education Community Outreach Programme in the north west.

CECOP focuses on the area around Buliisa, which borders on Murchison, Uganda's largest national park and one of its major tourist attractions. The project aims to reduce poverty through education and the promotion of environmentally friendly and sustainable community driven initiatives.

The southern part of Uganda has seen more development than the north and the north west in particular has a turbulent history. It is populated largely by the Acholi people, who are also found in South Sudan. The Acholi were well represented in the government of president Milton Obote who relied on them for advice, but Idi Amin who deposed Obote and was from the north but not Acholi, distrusted them and many were killed during his time in power. After the overthrow of Amin, Tito Okello, an Acholi, was briefly president until ousted by the present president Yoweri Museveni.

At this point civil war broke out between the people of the north, mainly Acholi and government forces. Several rebel leaders came on the scene and it seems highly likely that both sides resorted to war crimes including the abduction of children to become soldiers.

In 1987 Alice Lakwena set up the Holy Spirit Movement. An Acholi, Alice Lakwena believed herself to be possessed by the spirit of a dead soldier. Her followers took magic potions before action believing they protected them from harm. They marched into battle singing hymns and blessed stones believing this would turn them into grenades. Despite these beliefs the movement enjoyed some initial success and was joined by other rebel groups. Alice Lakwena managed to move her forces close to Kampala before being defeated.

After her disappearance another spirit led leader Joseph Kony appeared as leader of the Lord's Resistance Army (LRA) and was joined by numbers of rebel fighters.

What follows was a nightmare for many Acholi people. Museveni's Northern Resistance Army was undoubtedly heavy handed in attempting to quell the rebellion. Many civilians lost their lives and around ninety per cent of those who remained were forced to move into IDP camps (Internally Displaced Persons Camps) ostensibly to protect them from the fighting but also to prevent them giving aid to the rebels. Many were destined to remain in the camps for twenty odd years and only relatively recently have been told to go back to their homes and cultivate their land again.

At the same time Kony was also treating his fellow Acholi harshly, punishing them for any suspected contact with the NRA by chopping off ears.

In 1994 peace was negotiated between the two forces, but collapsed when Kony demanded six months to gather his forces together for disarmament. Suspecting a plot, Museveni gave him a week and the talks collapsed.

Kony received support in the form of men, arms and shelter from South Sudan, which was delighted to see its neighbour's northern territory destabilised. Then in 1999 an agreement was signed between South Sudan and Uganda and Kony moved to the Democratic Republic of Congo.

In 2001 George W Bush listed Kony as an international terrorist on a list which included Asama Bin Laden and two years later he was referred to the International Criminal Court at the Hague.

He is presumably still in hiding and from time to time rumours arise as to his resurgence. The truth is hard to fathom. Stories differ but one source of information, which I did find helpful was *The Wizard of the Nile* by Matthew Green, a Reuters journalist.

He makes the point that Uganda's problems go back to the north south division of the country and by demonising Kony, it is easy to ignore the genuine grievances of the Acholi.

Government forces were seen as saviours by the outside world while the picture of Kony as a religious lunatic, obscured the real issues. Both sides cited and continue to do so, the atrocities committed by their opponents and so justify the misery and slaughter and unsolved problems.

During the civil war the Buliisa area saw a rapid increase in population due to people fleeing the LRA and from the arrival of Congolese refugees escaping unrest on the other side of Lake Albert. Plus the area's own population was growing steadily.

Uganda has the third highest birthrate in the word, beaten only by Niger and Mali. Half its population is fifteen years or under and with only around twenty per cent of women having access to contraception it is calculated that forty six per cent of pregnancies are unplanned. President Yoweri Museveni sees the growth as providing a market for goods and increasing prosperity. He also points out

Uganda has the same land mass as the UK with only half the population.

Factors surrounding the formation of the Murchison National Park have caused further problems. Early in the twentieth century sleeping sickness carried by the tetse fly was detected in animals in the area. In 1907 it was reported that the disease was spreading to humans and between 1903 and 1909 the British protectorate government ordered a forced evacuation. Thousands of people lost their homes.

At the time colonial administrators were convinced this was the best way forward although subsequent studies showed few if any people had succumbed to the disease. The empty land was a perfect setting for a game reserve and in 1952 it was gazetted as Murchison National Park. To this day many local people consider the park as their ancestral homeland.

As populations shifted and expanded, pressure on land and natural resources increased enormously. Stocks such as fish and timber were depleted and communities were forced to exploit resources from the park.

At present households in Buliisa do not have a reliable food source throughout the year. Life is particularly difficult during the dry seasons, which are becoming longer and the arrival of rain less predictable.

In addition, large oil reserves have been discovered in the district and are currently under investigation, leading to local people being pushed off their land by both the oil companies and by powerful politicians and business people.

SPE is well regarded because over the past three or four years it has undertaken a school building and refurbishment programme with help from Leeds University. Education in the area has never been a priority. In colonial times the British found the area a rich recruiting ground for the King's African Rifles and had no wish for potential recruits to be educated above their station. Today many schools are community schools, which means they receive no government funding and consist of local people teaching children under a straw shelter or shady trees. For a school to be taken on as a government school and to receive funding, teachers and equipment, it needs to be housed in a permanent structure.

The CECOP programme was devised by Jami Dixon, who is now completing her doctorate at Leeds University with a thesis linked to her work in Buliisa. Managing the project is Maz Robertson, who copes with the heat and isolation by cheerfully immersing herself in work and by becoming a valued member of the local community.

CECOP began with a comprehensive survey of over five hundred households, which revealed a lack of income-generating opportunities and the unsustainable use of natural resources. Locals had resorted to illegal poaching, over-fishing and chopping down trees within the park.

The project centres on field workers selected for their knowledge of the locality. They speak the language, understand the issues in the area and work with community groups to design and put in place the groups' own initiatives. They train members to develop sustainable and environmentally friendly projects such as beekeeping, goat rearing and tree planting, so communities can build themselves and their children a sustainable future. The aim is for a group to have a short term and a long term project running together so the returns are spread over a longer period.

I go out on a couple of trips with Maz, the first one is answering a request for help from an orange growing project. The saplings are showing signs of insect infestation and the request is for repellant which the group will buy from the money allocated to them. There is a traditional remedy, painting the trees with nicely matured urine, but the group has decided against this. The saplings are small but I am assured that this type of orange grows more quickly than its Mediterranean relative. While it is not as juicy and delicious to eat, the fruit can be sold for orange juice.

Goat rearing is a popular choice and we visit a thriving project where members have fenced off a large area, where one billy goat and numerous nanny goats and kids chew away contentedly. Having believed that goats thrive anywhere it is a surprise to hear that they are prone to a number of diseases especially mange caused by mites burrowing into the skin. To cover this eventuality, the group has again set a sum aside to pay for veterinary treatment and the herd looks in fine fettle.

I haven't seen much of Uganda since my one and only visit to Murchison and so on the way back I decide to take a few days on safari.

My first stop is the rhino sanctuary I visited on my first trip. Originally there were six white rhinos. Now numbers have risen to nine with the arrival of three babies. One is called Obama because his father is Kenyan, his mother American and as someone wrote on the noticeboard: 'He has big ears and is going to change the world'. Rhinos only mate every three to four years and the gestation period is fourteen months so progress is slow and the hope is to import more ready-made rhinos from Kenya.

I book into Paraa Lodge on the edge of the river and am quickly rewarded with the sight of a lion hiding behind a hedge and an elephant in the distance. As soon as I open the car door a baboon rushes in and steals the packet of biscuits lying on the seat.

The lodge is dark with hunting trophies decorating the walls. It is easy to imagine moustached old buffers sipping their gin slings and comparing notes.

'Evening Horace, bagged a big'un today don't you know.'

After an early morning game drive and an afternoon boat trip I spend the next day incarcerated in my room dodging between bed and loo, unable to keep down even my malaria pill.

Once I am back in the land of the living I manage the long journey west to the Queen Elizabeth National Park. The first morning after an early game drive on which I saw about six lions and a dozen elephants, I go for breakfast and am told I must order cooked items from the waitress.

'Do you have a menu?'

'No you ask for what you want. We have everything.'

'Do you have scrambled eggs?'

'Of course.'

'And tomatoes?'

'What are tomatoes?'

'They're—tomatoes—red and round.'

'I have never heard of them. We do not have them.'

'Do you have bacon?'

'Of course.'

'Please may I have some.'

'Do you want your bacon inside your egg?'

'No thank you, just beside it.'

'If you have it inside it is a Spanish omelette.'

'What is in the Spanish omelette?'

'Tomatoes and onions . . . .'

'So you do have tomatoes.'

'Of course.'

'I'm sorry I thought you said you didn't.'

'Oh, that was the word you said. You say it very strangely. Say it again please for me.'

My safari leaves me with mixed feelings about game parks. Once again the animals amaze me, despite seeing them from a procession of vehicles filled with tourists waving cameras and binoculars. The parks are a great Ugandan achievement after the almost complete loss of big game during the Amin years and the civil war that followed. The downside is the effect on local communities. The parks are not fenced off. Deer wander off and eat people's crops while elephants can do tremendous damage. On the other hand if villagers' cattle wander into the parks they are coralled in and their owners must pay a fine to reclaim them.

Football

ACK IN JINJA I find myself delighted to be on familiar ground. It doesn't last long as I narrowly miss being mowed down by a matatu with 'Jesus Loves You' emblazoned across the windscreen, as it veers the wrong way down the town's only dual carriageway. A few miles up the hill in Bujagali, there has been another death, giving rise to renewed speculation about witchcraft. A young man of around twenty six dropped dead a few days ago. Rumour has it he was perfectly healthy, although there is a suggestion that his leg had become inflamed and swollen.

The dead man's family are close neighbours of the Bujagali witch doctor who now lives in a spanking new bungalow behind the high wall. To add to his income he seems to be offering home visits. A couple of tourists staying at Eden Rock went on a village walk with a local who took them to see the Bujagali. They reported that he was old and not very interested in them and the house smelt of ganja weed.

Soon after my return it was pre-school party time. There were two and each lasted about four hours so both volunteers, staff and children were exhausted by the time they finished. We played games, had a disco and cartoons and then the children had a festive meal of rice and meat before being given a present and an item of clothes. All the girls—over a hundred of them—received a knitted doll made by Jenny's mother. The girls were so delighted when they opened their newspaper parcels, they immediately wrapped up their babies in whatever they could find and walked around rocking them in their arms. Meanwhile the boys each had a ball and chaos ensued.

To finish off the week, there was the schools festival. I was up at 6.30am walking to the main road with the other stalwarts. We waited in the rain for around three-quarters of an hour for a lorry to pick us up. Around two hundred pupils attended the festival, which started with the Ugandan national anthem, followed by the Lusoga national anthem and then the Ugandan education anthem.

'We are Uganda's future marching forward through education . . . .'

Competition is tough between the twenty odd schools, which have visited the SPE education centre in the past year. Prizes in the form of footballs and exercise books are greatly sought after and the atmosphere is tense.

Security is tight as a couple of years ago a school was found to be fielding a team of bright young things, quick to answer all the academic questions, which miraculously metamorphosed into six foot muscle bound athletes on the football field. The school was disqualified, but the incident resulted in much ill feeling and must not be repeated.

I am timekeeper and answer-checker for the quiz, with a large clock in the shape of a teapot. Unfortunately I keep forgetting the start time so can't exactly work out when a minute is up. Teams are asked questions based on what they had learnt at the education centre including how to make a compost heap and the difference between fiction and non-fiction.

For the first time this year's event was organised entirely by Ugandan staff with muzungus doing what we were told. They loved it and so did we.

Towards the end of my stay, to my great surprise I bump into Claire the beautiful waitress who so cheered my first visit. She looks dusty, tired and dishevelled and tells me that she had been 'in hiding' because she has had a baby, who is called Anna and is now almost a year old. Claire explains she is living with her family and trying to put her life back together. She has been offered work, which she hopes to take up in the next few weeks. We hug and promise each other we'll meet on my return. It is heart breaking to see Claire so changed, but she is young and bright and I comfort myself that with family support and her own enthusiasm she and her child can have a decent life ahead of them.

While many babies are born outside marriage and a formal ceremony is beyond the reach of many, for those who can afford it there is a traditional path to be followed. The first step is the introduction where the families of the couple meet together and the groom's family gives the bride's family gifts to make up for the loss of their daughter. In the past this was a serious bargaining time with much argument between the parties, as to the worth of the bride, but nowadays the negotiations will have taken place beforehand. The gifts are usually rice and sugar, chicken and goats, but where the groom's family has money they will include cattle, chairs, sofas, televisions and fridges. If the couple already have a child the price will rise because the bride has proved her fertility.

There is excitement in the village as an introduction is to take place and many of the guests are travelling a long distance. Some of them arrive early and wander down to look at Bujagali Falls where one of them stands too close to the river, slips, falls in and drowns. It is several days before his body is found by fishermen. Another able-bodied young man is lost and stories of the spirits who surround the water hungry for vengeance multiply.

There is also the story of Sumia to be whispered around the village. Sumia a young woman with two small boys, is in prison in Kampala. The story goes that a friend of hers was working as a maid for the brother-in-law of a high ranking politician. Cleaning the bedroom she found a stash of billions of dollars under the bed. Unable to resist the temptation the woman helped herself to a bagful and headed off to Bujagali for the witch doctor to cleanse the money so it couldn't be traced.

Once in the village she met up with Sumia who agreed to help her disperse some of the money. Sadly the bewitching wasn't up to standard and the woman was arrested. Police checked her phone, found messages from Sumia and arrested her and her husband. He is out of jail and trying to raise the bail money for his wife. Nobody seems to be asking what the politician's brother-in-law was doing with a fortune hidden under his bed.

Money is tight in the village as prices rise and the tourists have not yet arrived. The bodamen spend their days around the boda station each one trying to spot a potential customer before the others. It can be difficult when three or four skid up in front of you, each one insisting he was first. Trade being scarce they have dropped their prices and are keen to wait in town to bring customers back even if that means a couple of hours in Jinja. They can only afford the minimum of fuel needed to keep their bikes moving. Once they have a customer, a favourite stop is a hut a hundred yards or so from the village where they buy a half litre water bottle of petrol.

I use Steve whenever possible as he drives carefully and both his mirrors contain glass. If he is not around I have a list of drivers on my mobile. Just about everyone has a mobile phone, often shared by other family members. The fashion is to have a musical ring tone. At present the most popular tune seems to be *Clementine* and *The More We Are Together* but I have heard a touch of class with the opening bars of Schubert's *Trout Quintet*.

Jenny and I are off to a football match in Buwenda, a neighbouring village, as guests of Teddy's family. Teddy works in the café next to Eden Rock and her brother is the captain of the Buwenda Tigers. It has poured with rain for hours and the road is impassable by boda. Normally we would cancel the trip, but the match is a big one and the Tigers are christening the shirts donated by the St Edmunds Pacers from Bury St Edmunds. Teddy finishes work and the three of us plus a couple of locals keen to make it home, opt for the one and only village taxi.

We are slithering down the hill in the mud when we pass a boda spinning round in circles, with a man running alongside trying to hold a semiconscious body on to the bike.

A hundred yards further and we are at the football pitch. We send the taxi back to take the injured man to hospital. The driver phones later to say his passenger had been poisoned, possibly with insecticide meant for tomato plants.

The Buwenda Tigers lose despite their new strip. We stand under a dripping tree watching the goals fly in, followed by the captain's vote of thanks and an invitation to the Pacers to visit Buwenda and see their shirts in action. Then we retire to a neighbour's house for a huge African meal. The neighbour is well known as a cook and does some catering and paper bead making. She is HIV positive, but has been on antiretrovirals for a number of years and apart from problems when she changes medication, is in quite good health.

Not all who are HIV positive are so lucky. David's story is all too common. After he was born his father went away to find work, returning HIV positive several years later. David's mother became infected and when his sister Eve was born she was also HIV positive. Both parents died and the children were brought up by their maternal grandmother. When David was sixteen his grandmother and his sister became ill. One was in hospital in Kampala and Eve was in hospital in Jinja.

The grandmother died and David stayed with Eve in hospital for a fortnight until she too died. Entirely alone he carried his sister's body home and waited with it until relatives of his dead father arrived and took the body away for burial on the family plot some distance away. Since then David has lived alone. He is lonely but considers himself fortunate because he is being funded to finish senior school. He just wishes he had 'family in my house to care about me'.

Mango flies

I HAVE RETURNED FROM England and I am installed in my new banda at Eden Rock. It is bigger than the old ones with a new bed. When I emailed to book, the owner replied that prices had had to rise because of the installation of wonderful new beds. On arrival I saw a group of men chopping down trees and sawing away at the trunks. When I asked what they were doing I was told to wait and see because it was a surprise. Fred the manager opened the door of my banda and pointed with a flourish to the bed which looked like the old one but slightly wider with a post sticking up at each end—a four poster!! I agreed it was great and sat on it appreciatively before pointing out:

'The mosquito net over the top looks a bit small.'

'Because the bed is so big.'

'But the net doesn't cover it.'

'The beds are excellent.'

'Yes but what are we going to do about the net?'

'We'll pull it down.'

After a few minutes of trying to get a pint over a quart pot Fred agreed the bed was so magnificent it merited a new net and sure enough it arrived the next day.

The bed itself is something of a mixed blessing. The ones made in the town have only a small space between the slats while my slats are more widely spaced. The mattress is a slab of foam, which after a few days has dented into my shape so I now feel the slats through it. As a temporary measure I am sleeping on the edge of the bed where the foam is still thicker but need to seek advice on plumping up foam.

Another luxury with problems is the hot water system. When I switched on the heater a scalding hot dribble of water trickled out of the shower. I turned on the cold tap which promptly fell away in my hand. Giving up I grabbed my towel and shampoo and scurried round to the shower block only to fall over on the wet gravel, grazing my elbow and knee and bruising my dignity. Luckily there was nobody around to see me lying on a pile of dirt praying I had no broken bones.

For years there have been plans to flood the beautiful Bujagali Falls as part of a hydro-electric power scheme and work is now in progress. Nobody knows when the dam will be finished or what will happen when it is. Blasting continues on a regular basis and rumours abound that the work is causing miscarriages and illness. On a positive note the construction company is installing a standpipe in the village.

It is the rainy season so people are out hoeing and digging their fields early in the morning ready for planting. The land is so fertile, the story is that a spade planted in the earth would take root and grow. Even so implements are primitive and the work is heavy. Although the rains have come, there is still fear of famine. Food prices have risen one hundred per cent in a year, which hits urban dwellers with no land. Ironically there is plenty of food in the markets but at prices people cannot afford.

Rising costs are put down to the increase in fuel prices, which many blame on the fighting in Libya but the increases have been going on for months. There is a very different view of Libya's President Gaddafi here from the one at home. Gaddafi and President Museveni are close friends and Libya has big investments here—such as the UTL phone company. The press blames the European Union for its intervention in internal Libyan affairs, accusing it of being interfering, oil hungry and hypocritical. Newspapers point out that nobody rushed to the aid of Rwanda during the holocaust because it is a small poor country with no oil. The general attitude is distrust of nations who are perceived to put their own requirements way ahead of the interest of African countries.

On a local level the bad news is that Cibbi has been refused a visa to come to the UK and run the London Marathon. He has been training for months, has a free return airline ticket, accommodation with a former volunteer and lots of sponsors who have followed his training efforts online. It would not be the first time Cibbi has visited the UK, but visas are now issued from Nairobi not Kampala and the belief is they have become much more difficult to obtain. Cibbi submitted details of flights and accommodation plus six months of wage slips. He was refused on the grounds that he doesn't have a bank account which few Ugandans have as they are expensive to run. The reason for the refusal was it seems that the visa office was not convinced he would come back. There is a limited right to appeal which is in progress, but Cibbi is mystified as there has never been a problem in the past and now he is virtually middle aged with a wife a child and a cow to await his return.

My knitting group is going well. Ten or twelve stalwarts have been meeting in Jane's garden a couple of times a week and their knitting has greatly improved. They have produced phone covers, which we need to sell and are now on to hats and dolls. Two local craft outlets have agreed to take goods on sale or return and they are also on sale in the SPE shop at the Amagezi Centre. The trouble is at present there are virtually no tourists. We also need to pay the women a fair amount for the hours they work while keeping the prices reasonable.

Ruth has become a leading light in the group. She speaks good English and is generous with her time translating for the rest of the women. At the age of thirty seven she has seven children and she and her family run a 'born again' church on the northern edge of the village. She is studying to become a pastor and goes on missionary trips to convert the Karamojong.

In addition to working with the knitting group I am working with Kara Blackmore who is finalising an SPE exhibition 'Murchison Memories' at the National Museum of Uganda in Kampala. Kara has spent a year working with SPE and the Uganda Wildlife Authority on the project, which is a history of the national park. Such an exhibition has never been put together before and the aim is not only to give tourists a picture of the park, but for it to provide Ugandans especially students and pupils with information about an important part of their national history. There is to be a gala opening of the exhibition in around a month's time.

The first day is not good. Kara has gone down with chicken pox and I am waiting for a taxi to take me to my doom or at least the dentist. I was chewing my way through nothing too disastrous when I felt an ominous crunch and there in my mouth was the side of a tooth plus a filling. I tried mind over matter but after a couple of days the hole was not getting any smaller and the twinges were becoming stronger and more frequent. I enquired around for a gentle, well qualified dentist with a hygienic surgery and settled on Basil because he had performed root canal surgery on Shaz's partner Juma who is still walking around with a face that works.

The trip involves five hours in a taxi to Kampala and back and a day out of my life, when I need the time to spend drawing up a list of guests for the museum opening. My only comfort is that I should be able to pick up the invitations as long as my driver can find the printer's premises on the opposite side of Kampala.

I arrive at Basil's surgery two hours early as traffic through the city was for once moving freely. If anything the treatment is more thorough than back home. Both sides of my jaw are X-rayed to see if there is any root damage. To my relief Basil decides that as long as the cavity is cleaned thoroughly, he can fill it rather than crown the tooth. He gives me a pain killing injection and waits for at least twenty minutes for it to take effect. We fill in the time chatting about Bill Bryson, who, we both agree, is very entertaining and then move on to VS Naipaul. I begin to feel less comfortable at this point. Sitting in Basil's chair I remember the only book I have ever read by VS Naipaul was *A House for Mr Biswas* which I didn't enjoy.

Luckily Basil's fingers in my mouth prevent me revealing my ignorance and he regales me with the story of Naipaul's quarrel and subsequent estrangement from his protégé the travel writer Paul Theroux. The relationship began in 1966 when Naipaul was writer-in-residence at Makerere University in Kampala and Theroux a junior member of staff. It survived for years until Naipaul, perhaps suspecting a relationship between his wife and Theroux, began to cool towards his former friend. Matters became worse when Theroux realised that Naipaul had sold one of the books Theroux had signed and given to him. The battle lines were drawn as the quarrel became public. Theroux called Naipaul 'depressive, a skinflint and a misogynist'. In return Naipaul described his adversary as 'a bore who outstayed his welcome', and who 'wrote tourist books for the lower classes'. It is deliciously like hearing gossip about one's neighbours and all too soon I am swilling my mouth with the pink water to be found in all serious dental surgeries, shaking Basil's hand and thanking him for a sound filling and lively entertainment. I wonder if he ever heard that a couple of months later Naipaul and Theroux had a public reconciliation at the Hay Festival in the UK.

In the taxi home clutching my pack of newly printed invitations, growing accustomed to my reconstructed tooth and congratulating myself on paying only thirty pounds for the work, I remember guiltily that the price however reasonable by UK standards would be completely out of reach of almost all Ugandans. In the village the standard treatment for toothache is to suck on a sugar cane stick.

Writing the invitations is time consuming and involves checking the full titles of dignitaries such as ambassadors and high commissioners. There is also the logistical problem of delivering them to the right place. I scribble away and await further instructions from Kara, nursing a niggling suspicion she is going to ask me to phone people for raffle prizes. I hate asking for anything however worthwhile the cause. Writing begging letters is bad enough, but begging phone calls promise to be a nightmare.

As if that were not enough I have to pluck up the courage to tell Robina in the knitting group that I have run out of wool for the second slipper she is knitting. I am already in Robina's bad books and she is a force to be reckoned with. Her family is wealthier than many in the village with one son managing the quad bike operation and one in the army. The younger children are in school and Robina is a councillor in a nearby village. Soon after my arrival she invited me to her home to tell me she had promised the women in the neighbouring village that a muzungu was going to set up a craft group which would make them all rich. I was that muzungu. I pointed out that I had neither sufficient yarn, needles nor time to take on any further groups. I also told her she had no right to involve me in anything without asking me first. We parted on reasonable terms, but I am definitely not Robina's favourite person and the slipper could well be the last straw.

Kara is up and about but looks far from well. After checking the invitation list I am dispatched to Kampala to deliver them to the great and the good in embassies, universities, banks and schools. I am staying with Hannah who now lives in Kampala during term time so that her two older daughters Lauren and Jordan can go to school. Maya who is nudging three years has tried nursery, but has decided wearing clothes and being indoors is over-rated.

Despite being such a power house and achieving so much in such a short time, Hannah is relaxing company and after the children are in bed we sit outside sharing a bottle of wine and a chat. As we natter I start to scratch a particularly irritating mosquito bite in the middle of my back and complain that while I can't see it, perhaps it has become infected. Recently the bite has become sore as well as irritating and despite dollops of insect bite cream aimed with difficulty in its general direction, the bite seems to be growing worse.

'It might be a mango fly.' Hannah says casually and pulling up my top, peers at it and announces that she can see quite clearly that it is a mango fly and she will remove it in the morning when the light is good.

Mango flies are skin maggot flies. Later when I look it up online I find the Latin name is cordylobia anthropophaga meaning flesh eater and that they are endemic across much of Africa. The mango fly lays its eggs on the ground or better still on nice clean washing spread out to dry. The eggs hatch into larvae and when an unsuspecting person puts on the shirt or uses the towel the worm burrows into a convenient patch of human skin and settles in for up to a week or so when it burrows out as a fly to repeat the cycle, often leaving a nasty infection behind.

Vaseline or oil rubbed onto the bite blocks air to the skin and encourages the larva to come out, but Hannah is an expert and in the morning, while I show great bravery, she attacks the angry looking spot and soon has a grey lump squeezed on to a piece of cotton wool. I am fine until the creature slowly straightens out and curls its head up. At this point I begin to feel decidedly queezy.

A good way to avoid mango bites is to iron clothes carefully, especially along the seams, but in Bujagali that is easier said than done. Being positive it is much simpler dealing with such incidents here than back home. I can think of at least four or five people in the village who would not blink at squeezing out a mango worm whereas a practice nurse in a UK surgery might have doubts. One volunteer found on her return home that she had a jigger in her foot. These nasty little sand fleas are very common which is why SPE puts down concrete floors in schools, to prevent bare footed pupils from being bitten as they sit at their desks. The insect has to be removed intact and when this was explained to a nervous GP the girl found herself being referred to hospital.

I resolve not to tell anyone about my encounter with the mango fly but it's too interesting to keep to myself. Just like stories of childbirth everyone has a more gruesome story than the last. Shirray's pet dog had over thirty mango worms and needed an anaesthetic to have them all removed. While Stella as a child had a mango bite in her ear, which she tells me, could have badly affected her brain.

Museum

*M*y NEXT TASK for the museum is the catering. Armed with *The Eye* a monthly magazine which publishes just about all the information one could ever need—from ballet classes to used car sales—, I phone the list of outside caterers. Not an easy task as it seems some of the caterers have paid for space for a year but in the meantime have given up their wooden spoons and chefs' hats and retired. I dial number after number with no luck before eventually finding three caterers prepared to give me a quote.

The brief is not straightforward. Kara wants food with a Ugandan theme, which can be eaten with the fingers—so definitely not posho and beans. One company has a set menu and is not prepared to be flexible, but I ask for a price list anyway.

My approach to raffle prizes, being so faint-hearted, is not going well. The weekends in Zanzibar or Johannesburg, which everyone dreamed of winning, have not materialised. So far I have a quad biking session and a meal at a restaurant in Jinja. I force myself to pick up the phone and manage a couple more meals in Kampala.

It's time to abandon my knitting group and my banda and move to Kampala for the final week before the exhibition opens at the National Museum of Uganda. Built in 1954 the museum stands in impressive grounds. Its history dates back to the early twentieth century when it was called Enyumba ya Mayembe or House of Fetishes and its exhibits were thought to have supernatural powers.

Murchison Memories has been given a large airy room at the back of the museum. When I arrive it is empty except for a couple of SPE staff painting its walls a spanking white. There are five days for a transformation. My first task is to get in a taxi and drive to the shop to pick up the covers for the stands.

The fabric has been woven at Kilombera, the weaving operation in Buwenda and is now at a tailor's shop in Kampala being cut to the right lengths with velcro stitched at each end so the fabric can be wrapped round a stand and fastened underneath. I set off with Iga my taxi driver. He is mine for the day and pleased to be earning a set amount. Iga has four children and I gather two wives, although one might be dead and I don't like to press the matter. All his children are at school, but in the holidays he sends them to his parents in the country to keep them out of mischief and to help their grandparents on the land.

The landmark to look for is a café called Fifty Cups of Coffee. Iga knows it well and drops me off while he looks for a parking space. My instructions say 'Down the stairs at the side and then left'. There are five tailors' stalls in a row. I walk along and peer inside to see if I can see the fabric I have come to collect. I attract a fair amount of attention and am soon surrounded by shopkeepers who want my trade. I mention Soft Power Education frequently, gesture to bolts of fabric and explain dark red, woven, green and yellow stripes, very soft.

'Would you like a gomez?' This is the traditional wrap around dress with puffed sleeves. 'Lovely colours nice and bright and big.' one of the tailors says, viewing me critically and extending his arms to emphasise the point.

Someone else steps forward. He believes his wife took the order and she is at home. I speak to the wife on the phone and realise she is not the one doing the work. I go back up the stairs to be hooted impatiently by Iga. He cannot find a parking spot and has been waiting in front of a European style hotel expecting me to arrive at any moment. The doorman has had enough of him. We must go or he will be fined or worse still the police will take his car away.

I jump in and explain the situation. We must return to the museum says Iga keen to be on safer ground. I insist there is no point as Kara may not be there and we have to find the fabric. I leave a message for Kara. Can she remember the name of the tailors, or at least the phone number? Eventually I get through to her. She is up to her eyes in work and none too pleased that her assistant has fallen at the first hurdle. The stall is definitely near the café, but perhaps further away than the ones I have visited. She can't remember much more than that. The number is on her phone and she'll look for it. Meanwhile why don't I just keep trying?

Iga spies a parking space and hustles me back in the car. When we get out about twenty yards from the first spot I notice another small alleyway full of tailors' shops. I wander along and come to yet another alley off to the left. Sitting at a sewing machine outside the first shop is a woman sewing some dark red fabric. Problem solved, nothing to it really. I ask Iga to help me carry it all and smile at the shopkeeper who smiles back and tells me the job is finished, well almost finished. His ladies have been working long into the night and I can see for myself all the work that they have done.

My eyes rest on the roll of fabric at the back. There is clearly some way to go.

'When will the job be finished?' I ask. "We need all of it today.'

The shopkeeper rolls his eyes at these muzungus, always impatient and in a hurry, rushing in with a job and demanding it to be finished far too soon. Reaching a compromise we take what is ready and I arrange to come back late in the afternoon to collect the rest.

The first section of fabric fits perfectly and so does the second. With the third there is a problem—the fabric is too short and the two ends do not meet round the stand. I try another length, which fits, but the next one doesn't and neither does the next.

It's far too late for any more fabric to be woven. Belated measurements reveal that one of the woven lengths was around ten feet short. Phoning Kilombera the mystery is solved—as it was a rushed job the weavers used extra looms and miscalulated the length on one of them. The tailors cut each length into the number they had been given.

I talk to Kara and find out that while some of the stands will have exhibits on both sides others will be placed against the wall. With some minor adjustments to display plans I manage to cover the required number of double sided stands. Then the task is to cover one side of the rest, so it looks fine. The stand itself is made of stiff white material. I try pins, which are not strong enough to hold the fabric. I then go on to sellotape and progress to masking tape. Nothing lasts for longer than five minutes. Finally I find a needle and thread and cobble the fabric together.

Standing back to admire my handiwork I catch sight of a line running across the fabric, about six inches deep and lighter than the rest. I rub my glasses and decide it must be the sun. I look again and see another. All the covers have lighter stripes across them. Different spools of yarn from different dyes have been woven into the fabric, hence the stripes. Again it's too late. Nothing to be done except hope the exhibits will conceal the problem.

The next day it is off to the supermarket or to be exact two of them to buy the drinks. The budget is tight and over-spending is not to be considered. An earlier trip has shown that while the boxes of wine in one place are around fifty pence cheaper than the other, its rival has boxes of fruit juice on offer at knockdown prices.

Iga waits patiently as I trudge from supermarket to supermarket. In between there are visits to the caterer and tests of ingenuity like finding double-sided sellotape.

Gradually the exhibition takes shape, the stands are positioned so the ones with forlorn backs are against a wall with small tables bearing books blocking the path of anyone who feels the need to walk behind them. The floor is swept and the loos checked for toilet paper.

As I am on call to do whatever is needed I have time to wander around the displays. I learn that archaeological finds suggest the earliest settlements were around AD 290 in the Murchison Falls area. Memories from oral history go back to the Abachwezi people who lived in the area south of the Nile for two hundred years before disappearing in the 1500s. Theirs was a rich kingdom with wild coffee, salt and iron.

More disturbing was the development of the slave and ivory trades. By the 1700s both were thriving. Traders would take slaves from as far away as the Congo and trade them for elephant and rhino ivory. Hunters were often paid in slaves instead of money.

Samuel Baker who discovered the falls in 1865 was accompanied on his expeditions by his wife Florence who seems on several occasions to have been the more resourceful of the two. The couple met at an Ottoman slave auction when she was aged fourteen and about to be sold to the highest bidder, having spent her early years in a harem. Baker aged almost forty, rescued her and they became inseparable. Despite his achievements Baker was not allowed by Queen Victoria to bring his wife to court as she suspected they had 'lived in sin' before their marriage. In 1872 Baker was sent back to Uganda to eradicate the slave trade, which was still flourishing. His attempts ended in the Battle of Msindi where nine Banyuro chiefs were killed.

An avid hunter Baker was in good company. Winston Churchill and Theodore Roosevelt both enjoyed rhino hunting in the area. In 1900 a licence cost only 375 rupees and authorised the holder to kill, hunt or capture any game. In 1954 Ernest Hemingway and his wife came to view the animals. Unfortunately the chartered plane carrying them crashed. They were picked up by a launch taking tourists to the falls, which brought them to Butiaba on the shores of Lake Albert and a rescue plane. Unbelievably that plane crashed and burned on take-off. There is a suggestion that Hemingway's suicide a few years later was due to depression triggered by these events.

Anyone wishing for relaxed entertainment at the exhibition can settle down to watch *The African Queen* starring Humphrey Bogart and Katharine Hepburn, part of which was filmed against the falls although sections showing actors actually in the water were filmed elsewhere because of the risk of actors being eaten by crocodiles.

Murchison National Park came into being officially in 1952 with the intention that 'People who are interested in animals might go and visit them in their natural habitats.'

In 1972 the park was closed under Idi Amin who banned international tourism to Uganda, but today it is reclaiming its heritage as Uganda's largest national park.

Visitors arrive and are greeted effusively by SPE staff, given a drink and pointed in the direction of the exhibition. A tall formally dressed Ugandan comes up to me and says in an imperious voice:

'Who is responsible for this exhibition? Who is the person who has done this.'

His voice is so curt and commanding I wonder if I should warn Kara before she meets him. I point her out in the crowd but suggest as she is in conversation, he might like to look around further. Unheeding he sweeps over to Kara and blocks her path.

'Madam' he says bowing low. 'I wish to congratulate you on the exhibition. It is remarkable, the best I have ever seen.'

Mixed feelings

*T*HE PHONE RINGS early in the morning on New Year's Eve. Back in the UK, I stumble for the phone and hear Jimmy, Hannah's father. She has been awarded an MBE in the Honours List for services to education in Uganda, her name having been put forward by the British High Commission in Uganda.

Phone calls and emails fly between the UK, Uganda, Australia and anywhere else that volunteers, staff and friends are spending the Christmas holiday. It is a tremendous honour for Hannah personally and also recognition of the work done by Soft Power Education in Uganda. Everyone feels a sense of achievement and elation.

Reality hits when I return to Uganda a few weeks later. Touchdown at Entebbe starts badly when I am screamed at by a massive female official. Apparently I am standing in the wrong queue, although the one she is pointing to has a notice above it stating quite distinctly 'East African Passports'. It makes me realise humans all over the world can be bloody rude.

Bujagali is awash with mud and the rains have taken on a life of their own. They started in September and have been so heavy plants are rotting in gardens. The roads have the indentations usually found on beaches after the tide has gone out, which deepen with every downpour. As a result of the wet and the damp most people are nursing colds and the children have hacking coughs.

As I unpack I find I have forgotten to move the pile of knickers from the chair into the case. I have only three pairs and little chance of getting any more. The only place in Jinja to sell knickers is the market, where they are all very obviously second hand.

Still feeling disconcerted I phone around and arrange to meet friends for a drink. Once relaxing with a view of the Nile and a beer, I start to feel better.

There is news galore about SPE and the village. After we have discussed all the obvious topics I remember someone else.

'Does anyone have any news of Claire?' I ask idly.

Nobody answers.

'The tall, slim, lovely looking girl, who used to work as a waitress until she had a baby. I saw her a few months ago and she told me she was getting her life back on track.'

'You mean Claire—her family live just outside the village?' Shaz pauses and looks away. 'Claire died.' she says quietly. 'She was about to start a job with SPE cooking for a group of volunteers. I rang her in the morning to check the times and by the evening she was dead. She'd had a massive haemorrhage.'

'Not Claire. She had a baby girl, but she told me she had plans and the future was looking good. She was a fit young woman. She can't have died just like that in a few hours.'

'We don't know but we think she might have had an abortion that went wrong. That would explain the sudden blood loss.'

I think about it. Claire had been living at home with her parents. Perhaps she had continued the relationship with her boyfriend but he had not provided a home for her. To have two illegitimate children would be appalling. Her family's shame would increase tenfold and she would be looked at with scorn in the village.

Abortion is illegal in Uganda unless the mother's life is at risk, so desperate women who can afford to do so, find a sympathetic doctor and pay, while the rest turn to a local woman or witch doctor. Methods include inserting a sharp object such as glass or wire, swallowing detergent, smoking or drinking local herbs. Is this what happened to Claire?

I feel sickness and guilt. I had so nearly asked her when we met if I could help. Why didn't I? So my boda was waiting. He could have waited five more minutes. I might have made a difference, but I didn't.

I visit her parents with my condolences and her mother shows me Claire's grave in the garden. A cruel end for a beautiful woman.

Jenny's company is a great comfort. Together we take on the battle of Eden Rock. Worried by the lack of visitors the owner is building a swimming pool, cutting his staff and putting his prices up in order 'to attract the rich market'. Jenny has tried telling him rich people do not like sheets with holes in, Blue Band margarine for breakfast or dog poo in the garden.

Power is in short supply in the village and Eden Rock has to rely on a generator which is used sparingly. By popular request it goes on at around at six thirty in the evening and off at around ten. If we are out in the evening our return is eagerly awaited and we just have time to clean teeth, locate torch and leap into bed before we are plunged into darkness. At breakfast if we need to use the toaster, the generator is switched on for five minutes.

At the heart of the malaise is the fate of the beautiful falls. They are disappearing day by day. The dam is finished and the water is creeping past landmarks that have been there for thousands of years. There will soon be a huge lake covering the rocks and trees and the falls themselves. Most noticeable is the stillness and quiet. Gone is the sound of rushing water, which used to be so much a part of Bujagali. Cynics say that the electricity produced will be sold to neighbouring countries and that most Ugandans will see no benefit. The construction company is offering training in sewing, hairdressing and agriculture to compensate for the loss of livelihood. It's better than nothing but I am not sure how many people will find gainful employment from it all, other than doing each other's darning and plaiting each other's hair.

I try to keep my eye on the positives. Amagezi Education Centre is the proud owner of a biogas latrine. Graphic pictures on the wall show exactly how it all works and if everyone co-operates there should be enough gas produced to run the kitchen plus liquid fertiliser for the garden. Four thousand tons of cow dung have been put in to kick start the operation.

My knitting group has given birth to some exceptionally good knitters. Outstanding is Lily who can look at a picture of a knitted animal and then reproduce it, reminding me of people who can sit at a piano and play a tune without any music lessons. Proudly and with graphic gestures Lily tells me how a few years ago she had her tubes tied under a local anaesthetic. A travelling medical team visited the health centre offering tubal ligation for women and vasectomy for men. Nine women accepted but no men took up the offer.

However Lily's dedication is causing a problem between Sarah and me. James one of Lily's sons has profound learning difficulties. For years he spent his days rocking in front of his hut screeching as people went by. He could easily be mistaken for a six or seven year old but is in fact fourteen.

Thanks to SPE physiotherapy he is now able to walk, albeit in a twisted manner and can feed himself. Despite visits from outreach workers who have talked to Lily about James' care, he is filthy most of the time and now he can walk, he wanders around practically naked. I defend Lily pointing out she has many children and crops to tend, but then Sarah retorts that she finds plenty of time to knit.

Occasionally women leave children with mothers, sisters, or older siblings, but the majority bring their babies to the knitting group and either lay them on a cloth on the ground to sleep or breastfeed them at the same time as knitting. As word has spread the group has grown. I have divided it into three: the scarf and hand warmer group of very good knitters, the beading group making purses and phone covers decorated with glass beads and the beginners' group.

I have tried to find an interpreter and was recommended Fiona who has just finished secondary school. She made it to the centre despite a tropical storm and was full of enthusiasm. She tried hard to teach people to knit despite being unable to do so herself and was full of advice such as:

'You should teach people to put on stitches first otherwise they won't be able to do it when you're not here.'

Feeling my instructions were woefully inadequate she took pains to embellish them. When I asked her to tell the group that I could take no new people, she added that I would be starting a new class the following week. Unable to cope with her creativity I paid her and suggested she leave early before the rain began again.

The group has started to make knitted animals and using pictures of animals as a guide, Lily has extended the zoo with an elephant, a monkey and a zebra. I have my eye on a young woman called Proscovia as a possible group leader in my absence. She is clearly keen, a good knitter and speaks English. She is liked in the community and polite and respectful to her elders, which matters here. She is usually first to arrive, helps me set up and quietly offers to help the others.

At SPE it is a quiet time for volunteers. There is Tony, a Kiwi is in his mid fifties, covered in tattoos including a map of New Zealand on his calf. He has so many earrings it is a wonder his lobes haven't given up the struggle and fallen off leaving serrated edges. He is weighed down with gold chains and is a great storyteller. Tony is unremittingly cheerful and positive and works hard at anything he is asked to do. Everyone loves him and he is a great favourite in the village.

Alexa is the most noticeable of the young volunteers. She is very beautiful with an amazing figure. She is from Texas and looks remarkably like Jerry Hall. A couple of days ago Alexa was in the office trying on SPE T-shirts. She must have tried six on and every time sought everyone's opinion.

'Does the green look better than the blue? Does it drain my complexion? Should I go for pastels given my blonde hair? I know red is good on me but is this one a touch too strong? Would the pink look better?'

An enthusiastic volunteer she may be, but looks and comfort are important and dressing gown, fluffy slippers and hair dryer are vital items of luggage.

Determined to cheer everyone up Tony hits on the idea of a competition. Based on the popular TV programme *Come Dine With Me* he divides volunteers into groups instructing each one to prepare a gala meal for the others. The first one is not a great success despite its sophisticated menu.

'Prawns sourced from the horn of Africa, turned out to be three frozen prawns on a lettuce leaf, with a main course of Yorkshire puddings from the supermarket flooded with gravy to disguise their incinerated bases.

A butcher in another life Tony manages to source a sheep for his meal. Proud of his achievement he regularly produces photos of the animal munching grass, so we begin to feel we shall be eating a family pet. The evening is memorable: a table under the stars set for twelve with flowers and wine glasses, tomato salsa and French bread to start, followed by barbecued lamb and roast vegetables, with baked stuffed apples and marshmallows cooked on the campfire then dipped in chocolate to follow. There is entertainment in the form of James from the education centre doing his night job as a drummer and dancer.

The evening ends with noisy musungu attempts to reach Ugandan standards of gyration and is hailed as a great morale booster.

Villagers are eager to improve their standard of living, to have some insurance against a rainy day and this has led to the formation of several savings groups. Members pay in what they can afford weekly and in strict rotation receive their share of the savings plus gifts from the rest of the group.

Proscovia has been saving every penny she can in the hope of one day owning a piece of land and building a house on it. She is due to receive a pay out and invites me along as her guest.

A gift is in order, usually in the form of rice, sugar or salt. Undecided what to do, I follow the muzungu habit of buying a card and slipping some cash inside.

Feeling conspicuous in a skirt, I make my way through the village to the house of the chairman of the women's saving group. Led by the music, I step inside to be greeted by around fifteen women, all dressed in their best clothes and dancing under a home-made pagoda, with lengths of fabric stretched across poles to keep out the sun.

In the centre is a pile of goodies: carrier bags full of vegetables and fruit, bundles of firewood and four chickens with their legs tied together. I am given a stool uncomfortably near one of the birds, which overcome with heat and misery, fixes its beady eye on me begging for release. There is nothing I can do except avoid its gaze and pray for its demise so I can stop worrying about it.

The chairman opens the proceedings. The language is Luganda, but the main theme seems to be that the group is doing well and four lucky people are to receive money and gifts. Accompanied by much applause the music starts and the first name is called. Led by her supporters, the woman dances around the room and her sponsors hand her one by one her envelope and her gifts except for the chicken, which is left flopping on the ground.

It's Proscovia's turn, together with her godmother we dance around the room. I join in the gyrating and arm waving, secure in the knowledge that no muzungu can see me and to everyone else in the room, dancing is as natural as breathing.

Four happy women clutch their gifts and the chairman makes another speech, thanking people for coming and encouraging the audience to go home and save.

The energy and commitment are palpable, yet by western standards these women have nothing. They live in huts with no water or electricity. Every day they cope with poverty and sickness. Their lives are harder than mine could ever be. Yet they find the reserves to laugh and dance, to support each other and to plan for better times.

They are amazing and I think of Maya Angelou's poem
Phenomenal Woman.

> It's the fire in my eyes,
> And the flash of my teeth,
> The swing in my waist,
> And the joy in my feet.
> I'm a woman
> Phenomenally.
> Phenomenal woman,
> That's me.

Disaster

My EFFORTS TO settle down in Bujagali came to an abrupt halt. One morning I woke at around 6am and after trying to walk across my banda, I collapsed on the bed. Lying still I tried to convince myself that if I closed my eyes for a short time all would be fine. When this didn't work I was forced to be more imaginative and phoned Jenny next door. She arrived with a new volunteer and they both pronounced themselves perplexed at the sight of me lying in a heap.

Within half an hour Dr Charles had arrived, heaved me into his car and driven away to the Soft Power Health Centre. My blood pressure was taken and found to be barely there, my pulse was about the same and I was experiencing severe pains in my chest. I was attached to a drip and a taxi was called to take me to Kampala to the heart unit at Mulago Hospital. I crawled inside the taxi only to find the drip couldn't be fitted in as well and we needed to transfer to the SPE vehicle. The doctor fancied putting me on the floor in the back but after a cursory examination it was found to be too filthy for human contact. Poor Rhys who had recently joined SPE as an intern after graduating from Leeds University, was co-opted to drive and looked paler than I did at the prospect.

We all piled in: Godfrey a nurse in the back with me, Jenny in the front to wave madly at the traffic. By this time one hundred pre-school children and around twenty helpers had gathered together at the centre for a party and waved merrily as I left.

We stopped at a garage en route to collect a drug, which had been delivered from a pharmacy in town. A discussion followed between Rhys and Godfrey about whether we needed to stop or whether the injection could be given as we bombed along the Kampala road. Godfrey won and Rhys pulled up out of the traffic.

Unknown to us Shaz had contacted Hannah, who with her years of experience as an overland truck driver, had alerted The Surgery, a small private clinic, and an ambulance had been dispatched to meet us on the journey. I was immensely relieved to hear from the conversation in the front seats that I would not be going to Mulago. My previous visits had not impressed me.

By this time I felt as if I had an iron band tightening across my chest and just wanted to curl up in a ball. Apparently this was exactly what I shouldn't be doing and poor Godfrey was constantly trying to haul me up while keeping the drip tied with string to the hook on the door.

The ambulance flagged us down about an hour outside Kampala and I flopped my way in. Godfrey must have been greatly relieved to have help. The ambulance was reassuringly full of equipment and the nurse quickly put another drip in my spare arm. Once at the hospital I had to be manhandled out of the ambulance and wished not for the first time that I'd been to Weight Watchers and had my legs shortened.

Plasters were stuck all over me and wires attached by press studs to a machine behind me. Dr Monica, a young Italian doctor explained I had paroxismic atrial fibrillation and one of the drips was now putting a drug into my veins to stop it. Apparently in Europe I would have been anaesthetised, my heart stopped and started again, which would have done the trick but as this option wasn't available in Uganda it would take a while for the drug to work. I felt a surge of relief at being spared what sounded like quite a risky procedure.

A nurse then told the doctor I was very seriously anaemic. Mild panic followed until it was discovered that the sample had been taken from a spot around three inches from the drip and was almost entirely saline.

The clinic was fine—very simple with strange mattress and pillow covers made from the mock leather I recalled seeing on dining room chairs when I was a child. Dr Stockley the director came in to tell me he had had a similar attack a few months ago a week after completing a marathon and that the condition wasn't terminal although it felt like two Jack Russells were fighting to the death in my chest. Being very gung-ho about it all, he had apparently speeded up his own drip and chewed on a few extra tablets and was right as rain in a couple of hours.

By late afternoon I was beginning to feel better although light-headed and very tired. There was no food provided so Hannah brought me in some marmite, cheese and pickle sandwiches and two chocolate bars. During the night a nurse made me a lovely mug of tea which I drank, while finishing off a Penny Vincenzi block buster. I had asked Jenny to pack my knitting, but she had refused saying 'You're bloody ill and you can't have it'.

I was still attached to the machine, which was disconcerting, because there was no power in town and the clinic generator kept failing. I tried to follow the readings but fifty-year old 'O' level General Science isn't up to 21st century medical technology. As my lung function seemed to be nil most of the time I was forced to conclude I was dead and the waiting room for heaven was remarkably similar to my hospital bed.

With delicious inevitability the day dawned, Kampala woke up and I polished off the last marmite sandwich with great relief. That afternoon I went by taxi to Msambiya Hospital to see Uganda's one and only cardiologist. Dr Monica had told me that being the only anything in Uganda was not always a mark of quality but that Dr Areola was well regarded and everybody dreaded him retiring. For thirty pounds I had an echocardiogram, was given a report which I couldn't read and told to go back to the clinic and start taking Warfarin straight away. The problem was that when the heart is not beating properly clots tend to form and when the heart goes back into rhythm these are shot around the body causing problems. As Warfarin is basically rat poison I presumed that if I were bitten by a rat, the rat would die.

Once I had my Warfarin I was allowed to go to Hannah's house to convalesce, with blood tests every day until I reached the level when I could be given a fit to fly certificate. It took five days to reach this point. I felt completely well and had a thoroughly enjoyable convalescence including a trip to the Uganda National Theatre to see a pantomime written by the same Doctor Stockley who had seen me the previous week. It was *Snow White* and the prince removed the apple from Snow White with the Heimlich manoeuvre squeezing her ribs and kneeing her in the back rather than with a boring old kiss.

And so . . .

$\mathcal{T}$HREE MONTHS LATER I am back in England, off the Warfarin and on to something milder. I have seen a cardiologist twice and armed with medication, declared fit to travel.

The cause of the attack remains unclear but research online suggests that Malarone the anti-malaria medication might be involved. Looking back I also realize that the previous day I may have become seriously dehydrated. It had been a dull day so I was probably less aware of the heat than when the sun was splitting the skies. After a cup of tea at breakfast and a Stoney's Tangawizi midmorning, I had had nothing else to drink except a beer in the evening. This may have no connection with the incident, but I certainly intend to drink copious quantities of water on my return visit.

My ticket is booked, the spare room is overflowing with balls of wool, needles and beads which I endeavour to cram into three suitcases.

I think back to the time I was packing for my first trip, knowing I needed to run, but having no idea to where. I go over in my mind my arrival at the airport and the taxi journey to Jinja: the noise, the heat and the jostling black bodies as the driver wove round overloaded bicycles and hooted his horn good naturedly at anybody or anything less than six feet away.

Overwhelmed by a huge sense of failure, rejection and worthlessness, my only comfort at that point had been that nothing could be worse than the life I was leaving behind.

So what had I found in Uganda? I had found acceptance and friendship; Hannah the visionary whose idea of repairing schools has led to thousands of people from across the world working together; Shaz whose organizational skills make dreams reality and who now has a family of her own with Juma and baby Aisha; Sarah with her team working to improve the lot of children with special needs; Maz and her outreach workers bringing new hope to impoverished villages; Cibbi with his wit and humour, his wife Mary and toddler son Chico, echoing his father's greeting, shouting 'happy happy' to every passer by.

Tarvine is now sponsored to attend the National School for the Deaf in Kampala, learning sign language and showing a talent for drawing. His mother Stella is running her own café in the village and his Aunt Mary is a qualified lab technician.

The knitting group awaits me with orders for dolls, bags and slippers. Under Proscovia's leadership it is thriving. Meetings have moved from Jane's garden to the Amagezi Education Centre and the group has a committee and bank account.

Jenny will be there running her English language classes, so the evenings will be filled with news of the day's events and plans for the future.

Then there will be the volunteers, the life blood of SPE, who have heard the cynics' words that they are 'wasting their time' but who come anyway.

There will be sadness. Ruth who was so energetic in setting up the knitting group is seriously ill with an aggressive form of cancer. There will be no Claire and the beautiful Bujagali Falls are now one vast lake with barely a ripple.

My days will start with marmite and margarine, Steve with his brightly patterned shirt will be sitting on his boda at the gate, ready to remind me that I need my water bottle. I shall tie on my scarf so my white hair doesn't turn orange from the dust, put on my sunglasses, adjust my rucksack and clamber on, taking care not to burn my leg on the exhaust.

After five hundred yards we'll stop at the hut to buy a coke bottle of fuel and then head off down the hill, past the gardens of maize, the goats tethered to the verge and the children laughing and calling on their way to school. The sky will be blue and all around will be the verdant growth, which is Uganda. The air will be fresh and warm and I shall know that I am home.

Lightning Source UK Ltd.
Milton Keynes UK
UKOW03f1800020614

232729UK00001B/1/P